Careers in Focus

Financial Services

Ferguson Publishing Company
Chicago, Illinois

Andrew Morkes, *Managing Editor-Career Publications*
Carol Yehling, *Senior Editor*
Anne Paterson, *Editor*
Nora Walsh, *Editorial Assistant*

Library of Congress Cataloging-in-Publication Data

Careers in Focus. Financial Services.--[2nd ed.]
    p. cm.
  Includes index.
ISBN 0-89434-387-4
1. Financial services industry--Vocational guidance. 2. Finance--Vocational
guidance. [1. Financial services industry--Vocational guidance. 2. Vocational
guidance.] I. Title: Financial services.

HG173.8.C37 2001
332'.023'73--dc21
                                           00-012761

Printed in the United States of America

Cover photo courtesy Gail Mooney/Corbis

Published and distributed by
Ferguson Publishing Company
200 West Jackson Boulevard, 7th Floor
Chicago, Illinois 60606
800-306-9941
www.fergpubco.com

Y-2

Table of Contents

Introduction

This guide to careers in the world of finance covers the accounting, banking, and insurance industries, which are discussed in detail in the following chapters. These industries have been undergoing constant change in recent years, primarily due to technological advances. Although the increased use of automation may cause some jobs to be phased out, there will be greater demand for workers who are knowledgeable about computers and information technology in addition to having financial skills and expertise.

Another important trend in accounting, banking, and insurance is the growth of involvement in international markets, particularly in Latin America and Asia. Those who have language skills and an interest in other cultures will have increasing opportunities to expand their career planning to other parts of the world.

Investment and financial planning services are also becoming an important part of financial services. The aging baby boomer population will seek advice from their accountants, banking professionals and insurance representatives and require their services to plan a financially secure future.

Following the chapters on the three industry divisions are chapters on specific careers within those industries. Each article discusses a particular financial services occupation in detail. The articles in *Careers in Focus: Financial Services* appear in Ferguson's *Encyclopedia of Careers and Vocational Guidance*—but have been updated and revised with the latest information from the U.S. Department of Labor and other sources.

The **Overview** section contains a full description of the job. Oftentimes, a career has a variety of job titles. When this is the case, alternative career titles are presented in this section. The **History** section describes the history of the particular job as it relates to the overall development of its industry or field. The **Job** describes the primary and secondary duties of the job. **Requirements** discusses high school and postsecondary education and training requirements, any certification or licensing necessary, and any other personal requirements for success in the job. **Exploring** offers suggestions on how to gain some experience in or knowledge of the particular job before making a firm educational and financial commitment. The focus is on what can be done while still in high school (or in the early years of college) to gain a better understanding of the job. The **Employers** section gives an overview of typical places of employment for the job. **Starting Out** discusses the best ways to land that first job, be it through the college placement office, newspaper ads, or personal contact. The **Advancement** section describes what kind of career path to expect from the job and how to get there. **Earnings** lists salary ranges and describes the typical fringe benefits. The **Work Environment** section describes the typical surroundings and conditions of employment—whether indoors or outdoors, noisy or quiet, social or independent, and so on. Also discussed are typical hours worked, any seasonal fluctuations, and the stresses and strains of the job. The **Outlook** section summarizes the job in terms of the general economy and industry projections. For the most part, Outlook information is obtained from the Bureau of Labor Statistics and is supplemented by information taken from professional associations. Job growth terms follow those used in the *Occupational Outlook Handbook*: Growth described as "much faster than the average" means an increase of 36 percent or more. Growth described as "faster than the average" means an increase of 21 to 35 percent. Growth described as "about as fast as the average" means an increase of 10 to 20 percent. Growth described as "little change or more slowly than the average" means an increase of 0 to 9 percent. "Decline" means a decrease of 1 percent or more.

Each article ends with **For More Information**, which lists organizations that can provide career information on training, education, internships, scholarships, and job placement.

Careers in financial services are plentiful and varied, whether you are interested in working for a government agency or private enterprise, as part of a large conglomerate or as a sole practitioner. You'll find the financial world to be profitable and satisfying, both professionally and personally.

Accounting

Structure of the Industry

Accountants and auditors prepare, analyze, and verify financial reports for businesses and government organizations. The accounting department figures profits for the company, prepares its taxes, and keeps track of the cost of running the company. The auditors check those calculations to verify their accuracy.

Accountants develop bookkeeping methods that allow a company to keep track of assets and liabilities at any given time and monitor any changes that occur over a period of years. Accountants or auditors may be required to establish a system that breaks down debits into categories of expenditure (money going out of the company) or periods of expenditure. The bookkeeping system depends on the goals of the business and the needs of its management.

Budgeting is another major responsibility of most accountants. Using past and current financial records, accountants forecast what a company can afford to spend in a particular area. This plays a vital role when company executives decide how financial resources should be allocated.

Because each company has very specific needs, most managers, especially in larger firms, prefer to hire accountants to work exclusively for them. Some large companies are so complex that they have several different accounting divisions. A full-time accountant may be referred to as a management accountant, private accountant, or industrial accountant.

Smaller businesses may hire a permanent accountant as part of the staff, or they may hire one who will work with them on a freelance basis. Some small companies may hire a specific accountant to work with them on a particular project, especially if that accountant is an expert in that area.

The auditing department also works on the books for the company. Internal auditors keep track of company expenses to make sure that financial information is reported correctly. They are responsible for evaluating financial information to determine possible fraud or waste. They may also be responsible for developing more efficient methods of operation or new safeguards to ensure that the company is operating efficiently. Auditors monitor the company's operations and bookkeeping procedures to maintain compliance with tax and business laws.

When experts set up an accounting system for a business or individual, the needs of the client must be assessed before the system is designed. Sometimes more than one accounting system may be required to keep accurate track of the company's transactions, particularly in large businesses.

A balance-sheet system lists assets and liabilities, as well as other financial data. This gives stockholders and company officials insight into the well-being of the business on a regular basis. An income statement provides an account of operative costs and cash intake, so the overall cost of doing business can be appraised regularly, without calculating in other company investments.

Accounting systems can also be set up to list earnings paid to stockholders and earnings that are reinvested in the company. The flow of funds can be tracked to determine where and when company funds are paid out. If there are periods when a large amount of cash leaves the company, then arrangements may be requested to reschedule payments to remove high and low points in the cash flow.

In a larger company, a staff of accountants will share the responsibilities of tracking the business. Accounting firms handle the complex finances of large corporations which require external assistance with financial management.

During the late 1980s, several accounting firms merged into larger corporations. The trend continues today; accounting firms are condensing into larger groups to cover a broader geographical area and to offer clients a wider range of services.

Industry Outlook

Through 2008, the accounting industry is expected to grow at an average rate. Technology will continue to change the face of the industry with the invention of complex computer systems, software, and artificial intelligence. Number crunching jobs will be eliminated, while those that require computer experience and analytical skills will be valued.

Look for more firms to merge in order to remain competitive and to specialize in an effort to find their niche in the marketplace. Firms will find themselves competing against other non-CPA companies for the same business and will ultimately seek their alliance to build a stronger business.

While mergers continue and staff, including partners, are cut back, smaller firms will flourish. The American Institute of Certified Public Accountants expects higher work standards to be established and more rigorous training and hiring of lower and mid-level workers. High-level employees will be phased out, and para-professional accountants, in-line with paralegals, will step in.

The outlook for accounting can still be considered bright, following on the heels of a radically changed banking industry, and the number and complexity of financial transactions continues to increase. Expect the accounting industry to grow in the following four key areas: international accounting, investigative accounting, environmental accounting, and financial/estate planning.

Banking and Financial Services

Structure of the Industry

Banking. Banks and savings institutions in the United States are financial businesses, chartered and supervised by either state or federal government agencies to provide financial services for the public. In the late 1990s, banks collectively administered hundreds of billions in resources and millions of dollars more in trust funds and other accounts.

Basically, individual banks act as intermediaries for the movement of money, credit, and capital to wherever they are needed within the economy. It is estimated that 90 percent of all payments in the United States are made by bank checks. In the late 1980s, there were billions of checks written in the United States each year, and the number is increasing steadily. In addition to checks, most banks today also offer debit cards. Debit cards look like credit cards but draw from the user's checking account.

Today, most automobiles, home appliances, and houses are bought through bank consumer loans. Inventories, equipment, and machinery for business and industry are financed by term loans made through bank commercial departments.

There are thousands of commercial banks, which are sometimes described as financial department stores because they offer all kinds of financial services, such as checking and savings accounts, loans, and trust services for the administration of estates, endowments, and pension funds. There are also several hundred savings and loan institutions in various states that specialize in savings and time accounts and the making of mortgage loans.

In addition to large banks and savings and loan institutions, there are scores of private and specialized banks, such as investment banks and land banks. Under federal law, banks cannot underwrite stock or bond issues. They cannot engage in underwriting or investment banking. But they can take and fill orders, and in 1982 the government began approving requests from banks and bank holding companies to acquire or establish brokerages. These limited service firms either perform their own market operations or contract with carrying firms to handle stock and bond trades, registration and billing, and dividends and margin accounts. The SEC extended its regulatory scope over the stock-brokerage activities of about 2,000 banks in 1985.

Banks operate thousands of offices located in practically every neighborhood and community in the country. Many of the larger banks maintain offices in principal foreign cities of the world. The banks are organized so that through correspondent relationships, they perform services for other banks or for individual customers both in this country and abroad.

The major service areas of banking are in commercial banking, including corporate lending; consumer or retail banking; and trust administration and estate planning. Business banking is the major service function of the industry. Business bankers are involved in making loans to businesses and corporations. This includes providing credit assistance for such things as accounts receivable financing, leasing, energy financing, and equipment financing. Bank loans to commerce and industry total hundreds of billions of dollars.

Corporate services also include foreign currency exchange and other trade-related requirements for companies that export their products. Such companies use special financing techniques, such as cross-currency loans and commercial letters of credit. International banking is one of the newer and interesting specialties within the industry.

Retail banking offers consumers not only lending services, but also savings, investment, and payment services. Mortgage loans are made for the purchase of homes, and smaller amounts are lent for appliances, cars, vacations, and the like through traditional installment loans or even a line of credit activated by a checking account or other means.

Bank cards represent the fastest growing type of consumer credit in America. Commercial credit cards, as well as individual bank cards, offer customers flexibility in money management and convenient credit availability.

Payment services for bank customers range from regular checking accounts to bill-paying services, 24-hour automated teller machines, and direct deposit of Social Security checks and other dividend checks. Most banks now offer debit cards. While they appear as credit cards and often are affiliated with a major credit card company, the debit cards draw from the user's checking account. The major advantage to debit cards over checks is the ease of use (no need to show further identification). Savings services include statement and passbook accounts, as well as a variety of long-term deposits offering higher rates of interest.

Bank trust services, which were originally for the administration and conservation of large estates, are now growing to include pension and retirement funds and a wide variety of smaller funds to meet the needs of people of moderate means. Through trust departments, customers may arrange for professional administration of their assets, estate planning, and a variety of personal financial services.

The Securities Industry. The New York Stock Exchange, the American Stock Exchange, and the regional exchanges (for example, the Midwest Stock Exchange in Chicago and the Pacific Stock Exchange in San Francisco) provide central meeting places and supervised auction markets where member brokers may buy and sell securities for their clients. The exchanges as such do not buy or sell securities nor do they set prices. Instead, they provide the facilities for trading and enforce a variety of rules and regulations designed to maintain fair and orderly markets. The exchanges require the companies that are listed to meet certain specified standards of size and earnings and to publicize important basic financial information regularly. All around the world, shares in companies that offer stocks and other securities are traded every business day.

The Over-the-Counter Market (OTC) is, after the New York Stock Exchange, the second largest U.S. market for stocks. It is served by a network of brokers; they are not in one specific place, as are exchange members. The electronic NASDAQ (National Association of Security Dealers Automatic Quote System) offers shares of new or smaller companies traded on the OTC.

The business practices of the member brokers are governed by rules requiring certain amounts of financial backing and strict standards of business conduct in their dealings with clients and with each other. Most exchanges are limited-membership associations, and admission is by election. Rules are established by a constitution and bylaws and are enforced by an elected governing board with the aid of officers and committees. At the New York and American exchanges, the supervisory work is carried out by a paid professional staff.

Specialists are those member brokers who deal only with other brokers and act for those brokers who cannot remain at a post on the exchange floor until prices specified by their customers' buy and sell orders are reached. Part of the regular brokerage commission is paid to them when they act as a "broker's broker." The specialists also act as dealers, buying and selling shares for their own accounts. It is their job to sell stock when nobody wants to sell and to buy when there are no buyers. In this way they maintain a market and try to restrain wide fluctuations in price.

The American Stock Exchange (AMEX) trades in the shares of smaller, growing companies. Formerly known as the Curb Exchange because trading used to be done out-of-doors on the street, AMEX served as the proving ground for trading in the shares of such companies as Du Pont, General Motors, and RCA, all of which subsequently transferred to the New York Stock Exchange. The regional stock exchanges trade many of the same stocks that are listed on the two major exchanges. The regional exchanges also trade the shares of many smaller local companies.

The American Stock Exchange is also a membership organization. The New York and American Stock Exchanges operate in a similar fashion. The president, selected by the board of governors, is charged with administrative responsibility, and under the president's direction, a staff of several hundred people implement policy. The Surveillance Department follows the action of market prices and studies financial news, investment advisory service reports, and brokerage recommendations, watching for any signs of unusual activity.

Self-regulation has characterized the securities markets in this country since their inception. The exchanges have always, in varying degrees, imposed upon their members certain rules of conduct. These self-governing activities were officially endorsed and strengthened by the first federal Securities Acts of 1933 and 1934, which set the current pattern of self-regulation supervised by the government.

Before the passage of the legislation that created the federal agency, the Securities and Exchange Commission (SEC), the individual states had enacted a number of contradictory laws purporting to regulate the sale of securities. These varied greatly and only a few provided for effective enforcement. Today, however, each state has some legislation governing issuance and sale of securities. Some have created smaller and somewhat similar versions of the SEC. They all require securities and brokers to be registered, and some have established qualification standards for salespeople. Certain selling practices are prohibited in some states, and the public sale of securities that do not meet strict standards can be prohibited by several state administrators.

The federal SEC bears the main burden of overseeing the operations of the securities industry, enforcing the laws passed by Congress in the interest of protecting the investing public. It is composed of five commissioners, appointed by the president, with no more than three commissioners belonging to one political party. Its staff is responsible for registering, supervising, and investigating the operations of the securities industry.

At the SEC headquarters, the Division of Corporation Finance examines the many detailed financial statements that must be submitted by companies that sell their stock to the public. If any statement seems misleading, inaccurate, or incomplete, the company is so informed and given an opportunity to file corrections or clarifications before the securities can be sold. The commission can prohibit the sale of securities if all the facts are not presented or if they appear misleading.

The SEC, however, has no power to pass on the merits of a security. It cannot pass judgment on value or price. A company that might want to dig for green cheese on the moon could be permitted to sell its stock by the SEC, as long as all the facts about this venture were truthfully and completely stated. Congress left to individual investors the responsibility for appraising the actual value of particular securities offered for sale.

Two out of three SEC employees are located in Washington while the others work in the regional and branch offices. College training is a virtual necessity, and the more important jobs require more specialized training. The SEC has been a noted training ground for many young lawyers who have subsequently gone into private practice.

While the individual exchanges supervise the trading on the floor and many of the activities of their members, the main responsibility for self-regulation of the over-the-counter markets rests with the National Association of Securities Dealers. This self-policing organization is a private, nonprofit organization headquartered in Washington, DC, with fourteen district offices. It enforces the rules of fair practice that govern the professional conduct of its member firms, and a uniform practice code that deals with technical methods for executing transactions and conducting a securities business. The bulk of its work is done by committees composed of brokers who serve without pay, acting on the principle that ethical standards can best be adopted and enforced by self-governing bodies of individuals rather than by direct government controls and regulations.

Surprise examinations are made of all member offices at least once every three years. Salespeople's backgrounds are reviewed and all must take special examinations, in addition to those required by the major stock exchanges. Underwriting practices are watched, and excessive price changes are reported and analyzed. Disciplinary actions such as fines, suspensions, and expulsion from the association are taken against those who violate the various rules.

The Commodity Futures Industry. Commodity exchanges in various parts of the country provide facilities and equipment for commodity futures trading. Formed as membership organizations like the major stock exchanges, they fall under the regulatory authority of the federal Commodity Futures Trading Commission. They have trading floors with "trading pits" or "rings," where futures contracts may be bought or sold. There are eleven domestic exchanges, with the major ones located in Chicago, New York, Minneapolis, and Kansas City, Missouri.

Organized in 1848, the Chicago Board of Trade (CBOT) is the nation's oldest and largest commodity futures exchange. It accounts for about half of all the futures trading volume in the United States. It provides facilities for trading in futures contracts (agreements to buy or sell commodities such as agricultural products, silver, gold, plywood, and energy sources) for its 1,402 members. The CBOT also has about 700 associate members and over 1,400 members in special categories, for a total membership of about 3,600.

The CBOT and another Chicago exchange, the Chicago Mercantile Exchange, account for most of all U.S. futures trading. Indirectly, the two account for thousands of jobs in support and ancillary positions, from telecommunications specialists to brokerage house personnel.

Other American futures exchanges include the Commodity Exchange of New York, the Kansas City Board of Trade, the MidAmerica Commodity Exchange of Chicago, the Minneapolis Grain Exchange, and the New York Cotton Exchange. Some exchanges specialize in an industry. For example, the New York Cotton Exchange focuses on cotton contracts, while the Minneapolis Grain Exchange specializes in wheat. Other exchanges may offer facilities for futures trading in live and feeder cattle, coffee, copper, and other commodities.

Futures trading is a means of providing protection against changeable prices in the cash markets. Users of the futures market (buyers of grain, for example, or the farmers who grow grain) minimize the risk of adverse price changes by "hedging," or buying or selling futures contracts at prices immediately available.

Industry Outlook

New mergers and job cuts in the banking industry are announced practically every week, and some analysts predict that consolidations will reduce the number of large national banks to a dozen in the next five years. More positions will be eliminated as banks automate more of their functions and shift toward electronic service, striving to keep up with emerging technology and remain competitive.

While the number of financial giants decreases, small niche oriented and community banks will flourish. Banks will become more product oriented, trying to develop a unique position in the market and distinguish themselves from competitors.

Expect banking to become more automated and electronic. A bank in Oregon recently installed an automated loan machine—a customer can walk away with a check or direct deposit in ten minutes. In 1995, Security First Network Bank became the first "Internet bank" offering highly secure computer banking technology to customers online. Today, there are many online banks which serve the needs of an increasingly computer-savvy public.

Look for positions in computer and information technology, sales and marketing, and research to grow while administrative and teller positions decline. As banks aggressively pursue customers, ideal employees will be able to utilize network and database technology to collect and analyze information on prospective customers. Employees with aggressive sales and marketing talents will be valuable assets. Order-takers are characteristic of the old banking world. Bankers must now be a customer-focused sales force.

American banking entities are going global and growing internationally, especially in Latin America and Asia. The assets of U.S. banks with overseas branches and subsidiaries have more than doubled from 468 billion in 1988 to over 1 trillion in 1996 (Source: Federal Reserve Board of Governors). Many major banks such as Citibank actively hire U.S.-educated Asians and Latin Americans to develop banking business overseas. The creation of the European Monetary Union in 1999 has created favorable business conditions and opportunities throughout Europe for American banking institutions. Banking and financial services professionals who have specialized language skills, a desire to travel, and knowledge of these emerging markets will advance quickly.

As banks continue to compete with investment firms, they will seek out finance professionals who can develop products for the corporate market. Investment products and mutual funds are a booming part of commercial banking. This will continue to grow as pending deregulations attempt to remove barriers between commercial and investment banking.

The U.S. Department of Labor predicts that the securities and commodities industry will grow by 40 percent from 1998 to 2008. Like the banking industry, the American securities and commodities industry is expanding to a global scale. The opening of new foreign markets will offer securities and commodities professionals many new opportunities. The aging of the "baby-boom" generation—and their resulting need for retirement planning and investment options—has also played a role in the impressive growth of this industry.

Employment in the securities and commodities industry—like most other industries—will continue to be influenced by advances in technology and telecommunications. The industry has become highly automated and, as a result, opportunities for computer professionals—such as computer engineers, systems analysts, and computer scientists—will more than double in the next decade. Conversely, employment of brokerage clerks will grow slower than the average for all industry occupations, and employment of bookkeeping, accounting, and auditing clerks will experience slower than average growth through 2008.

Insurance

Structure of the Industry

The insurance industry is divided into three main branches: life insurance, health insurance, and property and casualty insurance. Companies may specialize in one or all three types of coverage.

Life Insurance. Life insurance is basically a means by which one person provides for the financial security of others—usually other family members—in the event of that person's death. Using life insurance in its simplest form, a person pays an insurance company a small amount on a regular basis (monthly, semianually, annually) for a policy that guarantees that the family will receive a relatively large amount of money if the person dies while covered by the policy. However, many life insurance policies combine this form of protection with others. Some provide for the policyholder to receive a regular income after reaching retirement age. Some provide funds for a college education for the policyholder's children. Some will pay off the mortgage on a person's home if he or she dies or becomes unable to work.

A new type of insurance which is being offered by some life insurance companies is critical care insurance. This insurance helps defray the costs of treatment for cancer and other critical illnesses. With medical advances and more patients surviving years with critical illnesses, this insurance provides for patients and their family to keep on living instead of only providing for the family upon the death of the insured.

Health Insurance. Health insurance pays all or part of hospitalization, surgery, medicine, and other medical costs. This helps protect the policyholder against large medical bills in the case of an illness or accident.

In Canada and other countries, people are covered by government health insurance. In the United States, health insurance is usually provided by insurance companies or managed care plans, such as Health Maintenance Organizations (HMOs) or Preferred Provider Organizations (PPOs). Usually, an employer pays part of the insurance premiums for employees. The government helps defray medical costs for the elderly and disabled through the Medicare program and for the poor through Medicaid. Supplemental medical insurance is often purchased to cover some costs not covered by Medicare.

Property and Casualty Insurance. Property and casualty insurance comes in a wide variety of forms. It includes the different kinds of insurance that protect people from financial loss if their property is destroyed, damaged, or stolen. It also includes all forms of liability insurance—the insurance that protects people from financial loss if they are responsible for injury to another person or damage to another person's property.

Within the property and casualty field, there are several specialized branches, or "lines" of insurance. Some companies write all lines, while others write only one. In addition to insurance on homes, business places, automobiles, and personal property, this field includes marine insurance, which covers boats and ships and their cargoes, and inland marine insurance, which covers almost anything capable of being transported or which is used in transportation. Inland marine insurance covers everything from furs and paintings to locomotives and bridges.

Also included in the property and casualty field is workmen's compensation insurance, which pays a person for loss of wages and medical expenses if he or she is disabled because of an injury or illness connected with a job. Workmen's compensation also provides death benefits for dependents if death is due to a work-connected injury or illness. Fidelity bonds, which protect an employer from loss due to dishonesty of an employee, and surety bonds, which guarantee that contracts will be carried out properly, are other forms of insurance written by property and liability companies.

Agents and brokers deal constantly with the public. In addition to selling insurance policies, they are responsible for advising each client about the particular kinds and amounts of insurance that will meet the client's individual needs. In some cases, they also help settle claims when a loss occurs by working out a payment agreeable both to the policyholder and the insurance company. Agents who sell certain types of life insurance also may collect premiums.

Some agents are employed by a single insurance company and are paid either a salary, commission, or a combination of both. (Commissions are a percentage of the premiums paid to the agent based on the value of the policies an agent sells.) Many other agents are independent businesspeople who are under contract to represent several companies.

Insurance brokers are independent businesspeople who represent no particular companies but who may order policies from many insurers. Brokers represent the insurance buyer. They determine the buyer's needs and procure the appropriate insurance. Some brokers are paid on commission while others negotiate a fee based upon the amount of risk they assume.

Agents and brokers often specialize in certain types of insurance. Life and health insurance are usually handled exclusively by agents. Property and casualty insurance is handled by both agents and brokers. Some agents and brokers specialize in only one line of property and casualty insurance, such as automobile coverage. Others may handle a diverse range of business.

Agents may work in large offices with a number of other agents or in small, one-person agencies. Some work out of their homes. Many agents combine their insurance business with other types of business; it is not uncommon, for example, for a property insurance agent to be in the real estate business as well.

In addition to selling and performing services for their clients, insurance agents spend considerable time on paperwork, record keeping, and correspondence. Depending on the size of the agency, an agent also may supervise a number of clerical workers and sometimes a staff of salespeople.

Because an agent's income depends on the amount of insurance policies he or she sells, the agent devotes a lot of effort to finding new prospects and establishing contacts with people who might buy insurance. This frequently involves considerable civic and social activities.

Large insurance companies that use independent agents and brokers hire field representatives to promote their line of insurance. Field representatives make regular calls on each agent in their territory who handles their company's insurance. They instruct the agents on new types of insurance and changes in old policies. They help find new business and assist agents in examining their clients' insurance programs to make sure the clients have the right kind of coverage in sufficient amounts. They also encourage the agents to conduct vigorous sales campaigns.

Field representatives are, in effect, district sales managers, but they must be exceptionally good at getting along with people because the agents they manage are independent businesspeople and not employees of the company. Their job is to encourage the local agents to sell more of the company's insurance.

Because their job is to instruct the agents about changes in the business, field representatives must keep up to date on all policy changes and be able to explain them clearly and thoroughly. Field representatives frequently conduct educational meetings at which agents are informed about developments in insurance and sales methods.

After an agent fills out an insurance application with a client, the application goes to an underwriter. The underwriter considers all of the information available about the risk involved, and then decides whether it should be accepted. If, for one reason or another, an underwriter decides that the hazards involved in insuring a particular risk are far above average, he or she may turn down the application or may accept it, but reduce the company's risk by reinsuring part of it with another company. Some companies specialize in reinsurance. If the underwriter decides that the company should accept the risk, he or she then sees that the proper kind of policy is issued and the proper rates are charged.

In large companies, underwriters are usually specialists in a particular type of insurance. Life insurance actuaries, for example, study statistics on how long people live, what causes people to die, what types of people live longer than others. From those statistics, they can project how long persons in certain statistical categories can be expected to live—"life expectancy" is the term they use. They cannot, of course, predict when a particular person will die, but they can predict with great accuracy how long an average person of a given age, sex, occupation, and so forth will live. With that knowledge, they can determine the amount of premiums that must be collected on each life insurance policy so that the insurance company will have enough to make payments when policyholders die and still earn a return for the company.

Actuaries in the property and liability field make many of the same kinds of studies and predictions. They can predict, for example, how many auto accidents will take place in a particular area and how much they will cost. That enables insurance companies to set rates that will bring them enough money to pay their claims.

Not all actuaries work for insurance companies. Some actuaries are employed by industry associations that propose insurance rates for groups of companies. Others work for insurance departments of their states. Some are independent consultants who run their own businesses.

When an accident, death, or other loss has occurred, the adjuster examines the claim. An adjuster may work on a great many different kinds of claims. He or she may be required to estimate the amount of damage to a house that is struck by lightning, the cost of repairing a damaged fender on an automobile, the value of a stolen necklace, or how much income will be lost because a store owner's shop burned down.

The adjuster also may be a specialist on one particular kind of claim. For example, the General Adjustment Bureau, an organization that handles much of the adjustment work for property and casualty insurance companies, set up one group of adjusters to work only on losses caused by missile tests.

Many adjusters travel to all parts of the country and sometimes to foreign countries. Large numbers of adjusters travel to the scene of major disasters, such as hurricanes or tornadoes, which result in thousands of insurance claims. In such cases, the adjuster's job is to examine insurance policies to make sure each individual's loss is covered by insurance, to inspect the damaged property and estimate the cost of repairing or replacing it, and to work out a fair settlement with the policyholder.

With the pool of money insurance companies collect from premiums, they invest in the national economy. Insurance companies invest huge sums of money in government, transportation, and utility bonds, thereby helping to finance many public improvements and further increasing their own income. In addition, they invest in stocks and insure many home mortgages.

Industry Outlook

Faced with new competition and widespread underwriting losses in the late 1980s and early 1990s, the industry will confront new challenges in the first decade of this century. Major restructuring will most likely occur in the life, health, workers' compensation, and auto insurance lines. Costs for these lines have outstripped inflation for more than a decade. The overall health of the industry is fair: the United States Department of Labor predicts that the industry will grow more slowly than the average through 2008.

As the population ages, demand for life insurance should rise, as will opportunities in the life insurance industry. However, the industry is facing stiff competition from financial institutions such as mutual funds. Only those that can meet this challenge will prosper. Private health insurance providers will most likely suffer as more people come under group managed care plans. The health insurance industry also faces some uncertainty concerning health care reform.

Insurance agents and brokers held about 387,000 jobs in 1998 with 3 out of 10 agents and brokers self-employed. The United States Department of Labor predicts that insurance sales are likely to rise in the next few years. However, due to technological advances, fewer agents and brokers will be required. Using computers and the World Wide Web, agents will truly be able to accomplish more in less time. In order to stay competitive, an increasing number of insurance agents and brokers will offer comprehensive financial planning services as well as multiline products.

Many companies are aggressively expanding into the international market, especially into Asia, southern Europe, and Latin America.

Accountants and Auditors

	School Subjects
Business Economics	

	Personal Skills
Following instructions Leadership/management	

	Work Environment
Primarily indoors One location with some travel	

	Minimum Education Level
Bachelor's degree	

	Salary Range
$20,600 to $56,250 to $100,000+	

	Certification or Licensing
Recommended	

	Outlook
About as fast as the average	

Overview

Accountants compile, analyze, verify, and prepare financial records including profit and loss statements, balance sheets, cost studies, and tax reports. Accountants may specialize in areas such as auditing, tax work, cost accounting, budgeting and control, or systems and procedures. Accountants also may specialize in a particular business or field; for example, *agricultural accountants* specialize in drawing up and analyzing financial statements for farmers and for farm equipment companies. There are over one million accountants and auditors employed in the United States.

History

Accounting records and bookkeeping methods have been used from early history to the present. Records discovered in Babylonia (modern-day Iraq) date back to 3600 BC, and accounts were kept by the Greeks and the Romans.

Modern accounting began with the technique of double-entry book-keeping, which was developed in the 15th and 16th centuries by Luca Pacioli (c. 1450-c. 1520), an Italian mathematician. After the Industrial Revolution, business grew more complex. As government and industrial institutions developed in the 19th and 20th centuries, accurate records and information were needed to assist in making decisions on economic and management policies.

The accounting profession in the United States dates back only to 1880, when English and Scottish investors began buying stock in American companies. To keep an eye on their investments, they sent over accountants who realized the great potential that existed in the accounting field and stayed on to establish their own businesses.

Federal legislation, such as the income tax in 1913 and the excess profits tax in 1917, helped cause an accounting boom that has made the profession instrumental to all business.

Accountants have long been considered "bean counters" and their work written off by outsiders as routine and boring. However, their image, once associated with death, taxes, and bad news, is making a turnaround. Accountants now do much more than prepare financial statements and record business transactions. Technology now counts the "beans," allowing accountants to analyze and interpret the results. Their work has expanded to encompass challenging and creative tasks such as computing costs and efficiency gains of new technologies, participating in strategies for mergers and acquisitions, supervising quality management, and designing and using information systems to track financial performance.

The Job

Accountants' duties depend upon the size and nature of the company in which they are employed. The major fields of employment are public, private, and government accounting.

Public accountants work independently on a fee basis or as a member of an accounting firm, and they perform a variety of tasks for businesses or individuals. These may include auditing accounts and records, preparing and certifying financial statements, conducting financial investigations and furnishing testimony in legal matters, and assisting in formulating budget policies and procedures.

Private accountants, sometimes called *industrial* or *management accountants*, handle financial records of the firm at which they are employed.

Government accountants work on the financial records of government agencies or, when necessary, audit the records of private companies. In the federal government, many accountants are employed as *bank examiners* (See the article, *Bank Examiners*), *Internal Revenue Service agents*, and *investigators*, as well as in regular accounting positions.

Within these fields, accountants can specialize in a variety of areas.

General accountants supervise, install, and devise general accounting, budget, and cost systems. They maintain records, balance books, and prepare and analyze statements on all financial aspects of business. Administrative officers utilize this information to make sound business decisions.

Budget accountants review expenditures of departments within a firm to make sure expenses allotted are not exceeded. They also aid in drafting budgets and may devise and install budget control systems.

Cost accountants determine unit costs of products or services by analyzing records and depreciation data. They classify and record all operating costs so that management can control expenditures.

Property accountants keep records of equipment, buildings, and other property owned or leased by a company. They prepare mortgage schedules and payments as well as appreciation or depreciation statements, which are used for income tax purposes.

Systems accountants design and set up special accounting systems for organizations whose needs cannot be handled by standardized procedures. This may involve installing automated or computerized accounting processes and includes instructing personnel in the new methods.

Forensic accountants and auditors use accounting principles and theories to support or oppose claims being made in litigation.

Tax accountants prepare federal, state, or local tax returns of an individual, business, or corporation according to prescribed rates, laws, and regulations. They also may conduct research on the effects of taxes on firm operations and recommend changes to reduce taxes. This is one of the most intricate fields of accounting, and many accountants therefore specialize in one particular phase such as corporate, individual income, or property tax.

Auditors examine and verify financial records to ensure that they are accurate, complete, and comply with federal laws. To do so they review items in original entry books, including purchase orders, tax returns, billing statements, and other important documents. Auditors may also prepare financial statements for clients and suggest ways to improve productivity and profits. Internal auditors conduct the same kind of examination and evaluation for one particular company. Because they are salaried employees of that company, their financial audits then must be certified by a qualified independent auditor. *Internal auditors* also review procedures and controls, appraise the efficiency and effectiveness of operations, and make sure their companies comply with corporate policies and government regulations.

Tax auditors review financial records and other information provided by taxpayers to determine the appropriate tax liability. State and federal tax auditors usually work in government offices, but they may perform a field audit in a taxpayer's home or office.

Revenue agents are employed by the federal government to examine selected income tax returns and, when necessary, conduct field audits and investigations to verify the information reported and adjust the tax liability accordingly.

Chief bank examiners enforce good banking practices throughout a state. They schedule bank examinations to ensure that financial institutions comply with state laws and, in certain cases, take steps to protect a bank's solvency and the interests of its depositors and shareholders.

Requirements

High School

High school students preparing for an accounting career should be proficient in arithmetic and basic algebra. Familiarity with computers and their applications is equally important. Course work in English and communications will also be beneficial.

Postsecondary Training

Postsecondary training in accounting may be obtained in a wide variety of institutions such as private business schools, junior colleges, universities, and correspondence schools. A bachelor's degree with a major in accounting is highly recommended by professional associations for those entering the field and is required by all states before taking the licensing exam. It is possible, however, to become a successful accountant by completing a program at any of the above-mentioned institutions. A four-year college curriculum usually includes about two years of liberal arts courses, a year of general business subjects, and a year of specific accounting work. Better positions, particularly in public accounting, require a bachelor's degree with a major in accounting. Large public accounting firms often prefer people with a master's degree in accounting. For beginning positions in accounting, the federal government requires four years of college (including twenty-four semester hours in accounting or auditing) or an equivalent combination of education and experience.

Certification or Licensing

Certified public accountants (CPAs) must pass a qualifying examination and hold a certificate issued by the state in which they wish to practice. In most states, a college degree is required for admission to the CPA examinations; a few states allow candidates to substitute years of public accounting experience for the college degree requirement. Currently twenty-nine states/jurisdictions require CPA candidates to have 150 hours of education, which is an additional thirty hours beyond the standard bachelor's degree. In addition, twenty states/jurisdictions plan to enact the 150 hour requirement at future dates. This criteria can be met by combining an undergraduate accounting program with graduate study or participating in an integrated five-year professional accounting program. You can obtain information from a state board of accountancy or check out the Web site of the American Institute of Certified Public Accountants (AICPA) to read about new regulations and review last year's exam.

The Uniform CPA examination of the AICPA is used by all states. Nearly all states require at least two years of public accounting experience or its equivalent before a CPA certificate can be earned. The exam, which contains four sections, is difficult—only 25 percent of applicants pass every section they take—and more than nine out of ten successful CPA candidates in recent years have been graduates of four-year college or university programs.

Accountants who have earned a bachelor's degree, pass a four-part examination, agree to meet continuing education requirements, and have at least two years of experience in management accounting may earn a certificate in Management Accounting offered by the Institute of Management Accounting.

The Accreditation Council for Accountancy and Taxation confers the following three designations: Accredited in Accountancy (AA), Accredited Tax Advisor (ATA), and Accredited Tax Preparer (ATP). AA candidates must pass an exam, while candidates for the ATA and ATP must complete required coursework in addition to passing an exam.

To become a Certified Internal Auditor, college graduates with two years of experience in internal auditing must pass a four-part examination given by the Institute of Internal Auditors.

The designation, Certified Information Systems Auditor, is conferred by the Information Systems Audit and Control Association to candidates who pass an examination and who have five years of experience auditing electronic data processing systems.

Other organizations, such as the Bank Administration Institute, confer specialized auditing designations.

Other Requirements

To be a successful accountant you will need strong mathematical, analytical, and problem solving skills. You need to be able to think logically and to interpret facts and figures accurately. Effective oral and written communication are also essential in working with both clients and management.

Other important skills are attentiveness to detail, patience, and industriousness. Business acumen and the ability to generate clientele is crucial to service-oriented business, as is honesty, dedication, and a respect for the work of others.

Exploring

If you think a career as an accountant or auditor might be for you, try working in retail, either part-time or during the summer. Working at the cash register or even pricing products as a stockperson is good introductory experience. You should also consider working as a treasurer for a student organization requiring financial planning and money management. It may be possible to gain some experience by volunteering with local groups such as churches and small businesses. You should also stay abreast of news in the field by reading trade magazines and checking out the industry Web sites of the AICPA and other accounting associations. The AICPA has numerous free educational publications available.

Employers

Over one million people are employed as accountants and auditors. Accountants and auditors work throughout private industry and government. About one-quarter work for accounting, auditing, and bookkeeping firms. Approximately 10 percent are self-employed. Nearly 40 percent of all accountants and auditors are certified.

Starting Out

Junior public accountants usually start in jobs with routine duties such as counting cash, verifying calculations, and other detailed numerical work. In private accounting, beginners are likely to start as cost accountants and junior internal auditors. They may also enter in clerical positions as cost clerks, ledger clerks, and timekeepers or as trainees in technical or junior executive positions. In the federal government, most beginners are hired as trainees at the GS-5 level after passing the civil service exam.

Some state CPA societies arrange internships for accounting majors, and some offer scholarships and loan programs.

Advancement

Talented accountants and auditors can advance quickly. Junior public accountants usually advance to senior positions within several years and to managerial positions soon after. Those successful in dealing with top-level management may eventually become supervisors, managers, and partners in larger firms or go into independent practice. However, only 2 to 3 percent of new hires advance to audit manager, tax manager, or partner.

Private accountants in firms may become audit managers, tax managers, cost accounting managers, or controllers, depending on their specialty. Some become controllers, treasurers, or corporation presidents. Others on the finance side may rise to managers of financial planning and analysis or treasurers.

Federal government trainees are usually promoted within a year or two. Advancement to controller and to higher administrative positions is ultimately possible.

Although advancement may be rapid for skilled accountants, especially in public accounting, those with inadequate academic or professional training are often assigned to routine jobs and find it difficult to obtain promotions. All accountants find it necessary to continue their study of accounting and related areas in their spare time. Even those who have already obtained college degrees, gained experience, and earned a CPA certificate may spend many hours studying to keep up with new industry developments. Thousands of practicing accountants enroll in formal courses offered by universities and professional associations to specialize in certain areas of accounting, broaden or update their professional skills, and become eligible for advancement and promotion.

Earnings

Beginning salaries for accountants with a bachelor's degree averaged $34,500 a year; those with a master's degree averaged $36,800 a year, according to the National Association of Colleges and Employers in 1999. Auditors with up to one year of experience earned between $26,000 and $36,250, according to a 1999 survey by Robert Half International. Some experienced auditors may earn between $56,250 and $91,000, depending on such factors as their education level, the size of the firm, and the firm's location.

Public and private accountants follow similar salary increases, and generally the larger the firm or corporation, the higher the salary. In public accounting, low mid-level salaries range from $28,200 to $32,000, according to the U.S. Department of Labor, and upper mid-level salaries range from $30,000 in small towns to $75,000 in the largest cities with higher rates from the Big Five firms. Partners earn upwards of $100,000. Mid-level corporate accountants earn from $30,000 to $65,000, and managers bring in $40,000 to $80,000. Controllers earn an average of $85,100, and CFO's salaries can exceed $142,900.

Government accountants and auditors make substantially less, though they do receive more benefits. According to the U.S. Department of Labor in 1999, beginning salaries for accountants and auditors were approximately $20,600. A few exceptional candidates with outstanding academic records may start at $25,500. Employees with master's degrees or two years of professional experience may begin at $31,200. In 1999, the average annual earnings for accountants employed by the federal government in nonsupervisory, supervisory, and managerial positions was $58,200; for auditors, $62,500. Accountants in large firms and with large corporations receive typical benefits including paid vacation and sick days, insurance, and savings and pension plans. Employees in smaller companies generally receive fewer fringe benefits.

Work Environment

Accounting is known as a desk job, and a 40-hour workweek can be expected in public and private accounting. Although computer work is replacing paperwork, the job can be routine and monotonous, and concentration and attention to detail are critical. Public accountants experience considerable pressure during the tax period, which runs from November to April, and may have to work long hours. There is potential for stress aside from tax season as accountants can be responsible for managing multimillion-dollar finances with no margin for error. Self-employed accountants and those working for a small firm can expect to work longer hours; 40 percent work more than 50 hours per week compared to 20 percent of public and private accountants.

In smaller firms, most of the public accountant's work is performed in the client's office. A considerable amount of travel is often necessary to service a wide variety of businesses. In a larger firm, however, an accountant may have very little client contact, spending more time interacting with the accounting team.

Outlook

In the wake of the massive changes that swept through the industry in the last decade, the job outlook for accountants and auditors is good, with estimates of thousands of job openings created in accounting and auditing by 2008, according to the U.S. Department of Labor.

Several factors will contribute to the expansion of the accounting industry: increasingly complex taxation, growth in both the size and the number of business corporations required to release financial reports to stockholders, a more general use of accounting in the management of business, and outsourcing of accounting services by small business firms.

As firms specialize their services, accountants will need to follow suit. Firms will seek out accountants with experience in marketing and proficiency in computer systems to build management consulting practices. As trade increases, so will the demand for CPAs with international specialties and language skills. And CPAs with an engineering degree would be well equipped to specialize in environmental accounting. Demand for recent college grads is falling as firms seek out seasoned professionals with marketing savvy, proven sales ability, and international experience.

While the majority of jobs will be found in large cities with large businesses, smaller firms will start up and smaller business will continue to seek outside accountants. Accountants without college degrees will find more paraprofessional accounting positions, similar to the work of paralegals, as the number of lower- and mid-level workers expands. Demand will also be high for specialized accounting temps; CPA firms have started to hire temps to smooth out their staffing through seasonal business cycles.

The role of public accountants will change as they perform less auditing and tax work, and assume greater management and consulting responsibilities. Likewise, private accountants will focus more on analyzing operations rather than simply providing data and will develop sophisticated accounting systems.

Accounting jobs are more secure than most during economic downswings. Despite fluctuations in the national economy, there will always be a need to manage financial information, especially as the number, size, and complexity of business transactions increases. However, competition for jobs will remain, certification will become more rigorous, and accountants and auditors with the highest degrees will be the most competitive.

For More Information

For information on accredited programs in accounting, contact:

> **American Assembly of Collegiate Schools of Business**
> 600 Emerson Road, Suite 300
> St. Louis, MO 63141-6762
> Tel: 314-872-8481
> Web: http://www.aacsb.edu

For information about the Uniform CPA Examination, contact:

> **American Institute of Certified Public Accountants**
> 1211 Avenue of the Americas
> New York, NY 10036-8775
> Tel: 212-596-6200
> Web: http://www.aicpa.org

For more information on women in accounting, contact:

> **The Educational Foundation for Women in Accounting**
> PO Box 1925
> Southeastern, PA 19399-1925
> Tel: 610-407-9229
> Email: mmi@magpage.com
> Web: http://www.efwa.org/

For information on continuing education, contact:

> **Foundation for Accounting Education**
> 530 Fifth Avenue, 5th Floor
> New York, NY 10036-5101
> Tel: 800-537-3635
> Web: http://www.nnysscpa.org

For information on internal auditing and the CIA designation, contact:

> **Institute of Internal Auditors**
> 249 Maitland Avenue
> Altamonte Springs, FL 32701-4201
> Tel: 407-830-7600
> Email: iia@theiia.org
> Web: http://www.theiia.org

Actuaries

	School Subjects
Business Mathematics	

	Personal Skills
Following instructions Leadership/management	

	Work Environment
Primarily indoors One location with some travel	

	Minimum Education Level
Bachelor's degree	

	Salary Range
$37,300 to $88,000 to $100,000+	

	Certification or Licensing
Required by all states	

	Outlook
Little change or more slowly than the average	

Overview

Actuaries use statistical formulas and techniques to calculate the probability of events such as death, disability, sickness, unemployment, retirement, and property loss. Actuaries develop formulas to predict how much money an insurance company will pay in claims, which determines the overall cost of insuring a group, business, or individual. Increase in risk raises potential cost to the company which, in turn, raises its rates. Actuaries analyze risk to estimate the number and amount of claims an insurance company will have to pay. They assess the cost of running the business and incorporate the results into the design and evaluation of programs.

Casualty actuaries specialize in property and liability insurance, *life actuaries* in health and life insurance. In recent years, a number of actuaries—called *pension actuaries*—deal only with pension plans. The total number of actuaries employed in the United States is approximately 16,000.

History

The term actuary was used for the first time in 1762 in the charter for the Equitable Society of London, which was the first life insurance company to use scientific data in figuring premiums. The basis of actuarial work was laid in the early 17th century when Frenchmen Blaise Pascal (1623-62) and Pierre de Fermat (1601-65) derived an important method of calculating actuarial probabilities, resulting in what is now termed the science of probability.

The first mortality table was produced in the late 17th century when Edmund Halley (1656-1742) noticed the regularity of various social phenomena, including the excess of male over female births. Halley, an English astronomer, for which Halley's Comet is named, is known as the father of life insurance. As more complex forms of insurance were developed in the 19th century, the need for actuaries grew.

In 1889, a small group of qualified actuaries formed the Actuarial Society of America. Two classes of members, fellows and associates, were created seven years later, and special examinations were developed to determine membership eligibility. Forms of these examinations are still used today. By 1909 the American Institute of Actuaries was created, and in 1949 these two groups consolidated into the present Society of Actuaries.

In 1911, the Casualty Actuary Society was formed in response to the development of workers' compensation laws. The compensation laws opened up many new fields of insurance, and the Casualty Actuarial Society has since moved into all aspects of property and liability insurance.

Old Age, Survivors, and Disability Insurance, now known as Social Security, was created in 1935 during the Depression and expanded the work of pension actuaries. The creation of this program greatly impacted the development, philosophy, and structure of private pension programs. The American Society of Pension Actuaries was formed in 1966; its three thousand members provide services to over 30 percent of the qualified retirement plans in the United States.

The first actuaries were concerned primarily with statistical, mathematical, and financial calculations needed in the rapidly growing field. Today they deal with problems of investment, selection of risk factors for insurance, agents' compensation, social insurance, taxation, development of policy forms, and many other aspects of insurance. Once considered mathematicians, actuaries are now referred to as "financial architects" and "social mathematicians" because they use their unique combination of numerical, analytical, and business skills to solve a variety of social and financial problems.

The Job

Should smokers pay more for their health insurance? Should younger drivers pay higher car insurance? Actuaries answer questions like these to ensure that insurance and pension organizations can pay their claims and maintain a profitable business.

Using their knowledge of mathematics, probability, statistics, and principles of finance and business, actuaries determine premium rates and the various benefits of insurance plans. To accomplish this task, they first assemble and analyze statistics on birth, death, marriage, parenthood, employment, and other pertinent facts and figures. Based on this information, they are able to develop mathematical models of rates of death, accident, sickness, disability, or retirement and then construct tables regarding the probability of such things as property loss from fire, theft, accident, or natural disaster. After calculating all probabilities and the resulting costs to the company, the actuaries can determine the premium rates to allow insurance companies to cover predicted losses, turn a profit, and remain competitive with other businesses.

For example, based on analyses, actuaries are able to determine how many of each one thousand people 21 years of age are expected to survive to age 65. They can calculate how many of them are expected to die this year or how many are expected to live until age 85. The probability that an insured person may die during the period before reaching 65 is a risk to the company. The actuaries must figure a price for the premium that will cover all claims and expenses as they occur and still be profitable for the company assuming the risk. In the same way, actuaries calculate premium rates and determine policy provisions for every type of insurance coverage.

Employment opportunities span across the variety of different types of insurance companies, including life, health, accident, automobile, fire, or workers' compensation organizations. Most actuaries specialize either as casualty actuaries, dealing with property and liability insurance, or as life actuaries, working with life and health insurance. In addition, actuaries may concentrate on pension plan programs sponsored and administered by various levels of government, private business, or fraternal or benevolent associations.

Actuaries work in many departments in insurance companies, including underwriting, group insurance, investment, pension, sales, and service. In addition to their own company's business, they analyze characteristics of the insurance business as a whole. They study general economic and social trends, as well as legislative, health, and other developments, all of which may affect insurance practices. With this broad knowledge, some actuaries reach executive positions where they can influence and help determine company policy and develop new lines of business. *Actuary executives* may communicate with government officials, company executives, policyholders, or the public to explain complex technical matters. They may testify before public agencies regarding proposed legislation that has a bearing on the insurance business, for example, or explain proposed changes in premium rates or contract provisions.

Actuaries may also work with a consulting firm, providing advice to clients including insurance companies, corporations, hospitals, labor unions, and government agencies. They develop employee benefits, calculating future benefits and employer contributions, and set up pension and welfare plans. *Consulting actuaries* also advise health care and financial services firms, and they may work with small insurance companies lacking an actuarial department.

Since the government regulates the insurance industry and administers laws on pensions, it also requires the services of actuaries to determine whether companies are complying with the law. A small number of actuaries are employed by the federal government and deal with Social Security, Medicare, disability and life insurance, and pension plans for veterans, members of the army, and federal employees. Those in state governments may supervise and regulate insurance companies, oversee the operations of state retirement or pension systems, and manage problems related to unemployment insurance and workers' compensation.

Requirements

High School

High school students interested in the field should pursue a traditional college preparatory curriculum including mathematical and computer science classes and also take advantage of advanced courses such as calculus. Introductory business, accounting, and finance courses are important, as is English to develop oral and written skills.

Postsecondary Training

A bachelor's degree with a major in mathematics or statistics is highly recommended for entry into the industry, and course work in elementary and advanced algebra, differential and integral calculus, descriptive and analytical statistics, principles of mathematical statistics, probability, and numerical analysis are all important. Computer science is also a vital part of actuarial training. Degrees in actuarial science are offered by over 50 universities. Employers, however, are increasingly hiring graduates with majors in economics, business, and engineering who have a strong math background. College students should broaden their education to include business, economics, and finance as well as English and communications. Because actuarial work revolves around social and political issues, coursework in the humanities and social sciences will also prove useful.

Certification or Licensing

Full professional status in an actuarial specialty is based on completing a series of examinations. Success is based on both formal and on-the-job training. The actuary may become an "associate" in the Society of Actuaries after successfully completing five examinations out of a total of ten for the life and health insurance, finance, and pension fields. The actuary may become an "associate" in the Casualty Actuarial Society after successfully completing seven out of ten in the property and liability field. Most actuaries achieve associateship in four to six years. Actuaries who successfully complete the entire series of exams for either organization are granted full membership and the title "fellow." The American Society of Pension Actuaries (ASPA) gives seven examinations in the pension field. Membership is awarded after a candidate passes three examinations and has at least three years of experience in the field. Fellowship is awarded to candidates who pass an additional series of exams, covering such issues as advanced actuarial practice. The ASPA offers several nonactuarial certifications including Qualified Pension Administrator and Certified Pension Consultant, both of which require a certain number of years of experience in the field and the completion of a series of examinations.

Consulting pension actuaries who service private pension plans must be enrolled and licensed by the Joint Board for the Enrollment of Actuaries, a U.S. government agency. Only these actuaries can work with pension plans set up under the Employee Retirement Income Security Act. To be accepted, applicants must meet certain professional and educational requirements stipulated by the Joint Board.

Because the first parts of each society's examination cover core material, such as calculus, linear algebra, probability and statistics, risk theory, and actuarial math, students do not have to commit to a specialty until they have taken three examinations. Completion of the entire series of exams may take from five to ten years.

Students pursuing a career as an actuary should complete the first two or three preliminary examinations while still in college, since these tests cover subjects usually taught in school whereas the more advanced examinations cover aspects of the profession itself. Employers prefer to hire people who have already started and passed the first two exams. Once employed, though, companies generally give their employees time during the workday to study. They may also pay exam fees, provide study materials, and award raises upon an employee's successful completion of an exam.

Other Requirements

An aptitude in mathematics and statistics is a must to become a successful actuary, as are sound analytical and problem-solving skills. Solid oral and written communications skills are also required in order to be able to explain and to interpret complex work to the client.

Prospective actuaries should also have an inquisitive mind with an interest in historical, social, and political issues and trends. They should have a general feel for the business world and be able to assimilate a wide range of complex information in order to see the "big picture" when planning policies. Actuaries like to solve problems; they are strategists who enjoy and excel at games like chess. Actuaries need to be motivated and self-disciplined to concentrate on detailed work, especially under stress, and to undertake the rigorous study for licensing examinations.

Exploring

If you think you are interested in the actuarial field try pursuing extracurricular opportunities which allow you to practice strategic thinking and problem solving skills; these may include the school chess club, math club, or investment club. Other activities which foster leadership and management, such as student council positions, will also be beneficial. Any kind of business or research-oriented summer or part-time experience will be valuable, especially with a CPA or a law firm.

There are more than 45 local actuarial clubs and regional affiliates throughout the United States, which offer opportunities for informal discussion and networking. Talk with people in the field to better understand the nature of the work, and utilize the association's resources to learn more about the field. The Society of Actuaries offers free educational publications.

College undergraduates can take advantage of summer internships and employment in insurance companies and consulting firms. Students will have the chance to rotate among jobs to learn various actuarial operations and different phases of insurance work.

Employers

There are approximately 16,000 actuaries employed in the United States. The insurance industry employs about 50 percent of this number. Other actuaries work for service providing firms—such as management and public relations, and actuarial consulting services—and in academia. Other actuaries are self-employed.

Starting Out

The best way to enter this field is by taking the necessary beginning examinations while still in college. Once students have graduated and passed these exams, they are in a very good position to apply for entry-level jobs in the field and can command higher starting salaries. Some college students organize interviews and find jobs through their college placement office while others interview with firms recruiting on campus. Many firms offer summer and year-round actuarial training programs or internships which may result in a full-time job.

Beginning actuaries may prepare calculations for actuarial tables or work with policy settlements or funds. With experience, they may prepare correspondence, reports, and research. Beginners who have already passed the preliminary exams often start with more responsibility and higher pay.

Advancement

Advancement within the profession to assistant, associate, or *chief actuary* greatly depends upon the individual's on-the-job performance, competence on the actuarial examinations, and leadership capabilities.

Some actuaries qualify for administrative positions in underwriting, accounting, or investment because of their broad business knowledge and specific insurance experience. Because their judgement is so valuable, actuaries may advance to administrative or executive positions, such as head of a department, vice-president or president of a company, manager of an insurance rating bureau, partner in a consulting firm, or, possibly, state insurance commissioner. Actuaries with management skills and a strong business background may move into other areas including marketing, advertising, and planning.

Earnings

Starting salaries for actuaries with bachelor's degrees in mathematics or actuarial science averaged $37,300 in 1999, according to a survey conducted by the National Association of Colleges and Employers. New college graduates who have not passed any actuarial examinations earn slightly less. Insurance companies and consulting firms offer merit increases or bonuses to those who pass examinations. According to a 1998 survey done by the Life Office Management Association, entry-level actuaries with the largest U.S. companies earned approximately $41,500. Associate actuaries with such companies earned approximately $88,000. Experienced actuaries in large companies earned an average of $101,600. Actuaries receive paid vacations, health and life insurance, pension plans, and other fringe benefits.

Work Environment

Actuaries spend much of their 40-hour workweek behind a desk poring over facts and figures, although some travel to various units of the organization or to other businesses. This is especially true of the consulting actuary, who will most likely work longer hours. Consulting actuaries tend to have more diverse work and more personal interaction in working with a variety of clients. Though the work can be stressful and demands intense concentration and attention to detail, actuaries find their jobs to be rewarding and satisfying and feel that they make a direct and positive impact on people's lives.

Outlook

The U.S. Department of Labor predicts slower than average growth for the actuary field through 2008. Growth of the insurance industry—traditionally the leading employer of actuaries—has slowed, and many firms are downsizing and even merging to reduce expenditures. Competition for entry-level jobs will remain stiff, as favorable publicity about the profession has drawn a large number of new workers.

Consulting actuaries should enjoy a stronger employment outlook than their counterparts in the insurance industry as many large corporations increasingly rely on consultants to handle actuarial work that was formerly done in-house.

The insurance industry continues to evolve, and actuaries will be in demand to establish rates in several new areas of coverage including prepaid legal, dental, and kidnapping insurance. In many cases, actuarial data that have been supplied by rating bureaus are now being developed in new actuarial departments created in companies affected by states' new competitive rating laws. Other new areas of insurance coverage that will involve actuaries include product and pollution liability insurance, as well as greater workers' compensation and medical malpractice coverage. Insurers will be calling on actuaries to help them respond to new state and federal regulations while cutting costs, especially in the areas of pension reform and no-fault automobile insurance. In the future, actuaries will also be employed by non-insurance businesses or will work in business- and investment-related fields. Some are already working in banking and finance.

Actuaries will be needed to assess the financial impact of health problems such as AIDS and the changing health care system. As demographics change, people live and work longer, and as medicine advances, actuaries will need to reexamine the probabilities of death, sickness, and retirement.

Casualty actuaries will find more work as companies find themselves held responsible for product liability. In the wake of recent environmental disasters, there will also be a growing need to evaluate environmental risk.

As business goes global, it presents a whole new set of risks and problems as economies develop and new markets emerge. As private enterprise expands in the former Soviet Union, how does a company determine the risk of opening, say, an ice cream shop in Siberia?

Actuaries are no longer just mathematical experts. With their unique combination of analytical and business skills, their role is expanding as they become broad-based business professionals solving social as well as financial problems.

For More Information

For general information about actuary careers, contact:

American Academy of Actuaries
1100 17th Street, NW, Seventh Floor
Washington, DC 20036
Web: http://www.actuary.org/

For information about continuing education and professional designations, contact:

American Society of Pension Actuaries
4245 North Fairfax Drive, Suite 750
Arlington, VA 22203-1619
Tel: 703-516-9300
Email: ASPA@aspa.org
Web: http://www.aspa.org/

The Career Information section of the CAS Web site offers comprehensive information on the career of actuary.

Casualty Actuarial Society (CAS)
1100 North Glebe Road, Suite 600
Arlington, VA 22201
Tel: 703-276-3100
Email: office@casact.org
Web: http://www.casact.org

For information about continuing education and professional designations, contact:

Society of Actuaries
475 North Martingale Road, Suite 800
Schaumburg, IL 60173-2226
Tel: 847-706-3500
Web: http://www.soa.org

Bank Examiners

School Subjects	English Mathematics
Personal Skills	Communication/ideas Leadership/management
Work Environment	Primarily indoors One location with some travel
Minimum Education Level	Bachelor's degree
Salary Range	$21,370 to $65,680 to $108,000+
Certification or Licensing	Required
Outlook	About as fast as the average

Overview

Bank examiners investigate financial institutions to ensure their safety and soundness and to enforce federal and state laws. They arrange audits, review policies and procedures, study documents, and interview managers and employees. They prepare detailed reports that can be used to strengthen banks.

A bank examiner's fundamental duty is to make sure people do not lose the money they have entrusted to banks. Bank examiners protect account holders. They also protect the federal and state governments that are responsible for insuring financial institutions.

History

The First Bank of the United States, founded in Philadelphia in 1791, was an unqualified success. It acted as the federal government's banker and received private and business deposits. The bank issued banknotes that could be exchanged for gold and succeeded in creating a national currency. In 1811, the visionary experiment came to an untimely end; despite the bank's many successes, its charter was not renewed. In a time when state's rights were considered supreme, a national bank was an unpopular idea.

The second national bank fared just as well—and no better. Despite an impressive list of achievements, the bank failed when President Andrew Jackson (1767-1845) vetoed its charter renewal.

For the next several decades, the nation adhered to a system of "free banking," meaning that bank charters were readily granted to groups that met limited standards. The number of state banks multiplied rapidly. Each state bank issued its own banknotes, creating an untenable currency system.

In the 1860s, the U.S. Civil War destroyed the South's economy. Banks in the southern states did not have the resources to weather the difficulties. The only national financial organization, the Independent Treasury, was ill-equipped to meet the ensuing financial demands. The price of "free banking" became painfully clear.

In 1864, as the nation struggled to rebuild itself, the federal government passed the National Bank Act. Intended to bring about economic stability and prevent future bank failures, the act created the Office of the Comptroller of the Currency (OCC). The OCC initially had the power to charter national banks that could issue national banknotes. The OCC also was the first organization to conduct bank examinations.

Unfortunately, the National Bank Act of 1864 did not bring about the desired stability. Over the next several decades, the country experienced four bank panics, the worst of which occurred in 1907. Bank panics were characterized by "runs on the banks," during which people became fearful and tried to withdraw all their money, all at once. The banks often did not have enough cash in reserve and many failed. The Federal Reserve Act (1913) created a centralized reserve system that could lend banks money and prevent bank crises.

In its early form, the Federal Reserve System was unable to prevent the bank failures that led, in 1929, to the Great Depression. In 1933, in response to the Depression, the Federal Reserve's powers were extended. The Federal Reserve eventually would become a central bank that actively promoted monetary stability. Like the OCC, the Federal Reserve now regularly examines banks.

The Federal Deposit Insurance Corporation (FDIC) also was created in 1933. The FDIC pays depositors if an insured bank closes without the resources to repay people their money. The FDIC also is charged with the responsibility of preventing unsound banking practices within the banks it insures. The FDIC regularly examines all the banks it insures in order to ensure their safety and soundness. Since its creation, the FDIC has successfully prevented any widespread bank panics.

The years since 1933 have not been without challenges, however. In the mid 1980s, hundreds of savings and loan banks failed, reinforcing the need for the regular, thorough examination of banks by the OCC, the Federal Reserve, the FDIC, and a number of other federal and state agencies. Most banks today are examined on an annual basis, often by more than one regulatory organization.

The Job

When most people think of bank examiners, they envision the examiner from *It's a Wonderful Life*—a humorless bureaucrat who threatens to destroy George Bailey. In reality, bank examiners are public servants. They work to ensure that our nation's banks remain strong and safe. Essentially, they protect our money and our nation's economy.

A bank examiner's primary responsibilities are to ensure the safety and soundness of the bank he or she examines and to enforce the rules and regulations of the state or federal organization he or she represents. To accomplish this, bank examiners travel to different banks throughout the year. In most small- to medium-sized banks, they set up temporary offices. In larger banks, they may have permanent offices. The examination process can take anywhere from a few weeks to several months, depending on the size of the bank. A few extremely large banks are examined constantly throughout the year.

Bank examiners should not be confused with auditors or accountants. A bank examiner is as interested in a bank's operations as in the bank's financial records. Bank examiners conduct their examinations by reviewing a bank's policies to see, first of all, whether the policies are sound. They then review the bank's records to discover whether the bank is following its own policies. Bank examiners also observe the bank's day-to-day operations and interview managers and employees.

Ed Seifried, who served as a bank examiner within the OCC for more than 25 years, notes, "Bank examinations should involve dialogue and discussion. Banks may not like the process [of being examined], but they generally accept it if they feel that they are being assessed by people who treat them fairly and who understand banking."

Bank examiners usually work in teams under one bank-examiner-in-charge. Each member or group within a team studies a different area of the bank's operations. One person or group might study the bank's lending policies and procedures. Another might study the bank's asset management. Still others examine the bank's information technology or estate management.

Different regulatory agencies examine different types of banks and different areas of operation. The *chief bank examiner* is responsible for assembling the team for each bank. The composition of these teams varies depending on the nature of each bank's business. Because banking practices today are so complex, many regulatory organizations design their examination strategy around a bank's greatest areas of risk. This so-called "supervision by risk" enables regulatory organizations to examine banks more frequently and with greater efficiency.

"Every examination is tailored to the individual bank," says Seifried. "The person in charge of the exam studies the bank in advance in order to develop an examination strategy."

Once a team of examiners has thoroughly reviewed different areas of a bank's operations, they analyze their findings, draw conclusions, and prepare a report. This report is forwarded to the regulatory agency for review. It is then returned to the bank's Board of Directors. These reports wield considerable power. A bank must act quickly to correct any problems identified in an examination. If a bank fails to do so, bank examiners have the authority to exact fines. In severe cases, a bank examiner can close banks or insist that they merge with other, more sound banks.

Because bank examiners must be able to exercise completely independent judgment about a bank's operations, their reports are strictly confidential. "The confidentiality is to ensure that there is no interference with the regulatory process," Seifried explains. "If bank examiners could be sued for rendering judgments, they might not be able to be as objective."

Requirements

High School

If you are interested in entering this profession, you should begin laying a solid college prep foundation during high school. Take math courses, such as algebra and geometry, statistics, and business courses. Also, take as many computer courses as you can. You will be using computers throughout your career, and the more comfortable you are with this tool the better. You should also take English classes to develop good writing and communication skills. Researching, compiling reports, and presenting your findings will be a large part of your job as a bank examiner.

Postsecondary Training

After high school, the next step on your road to becoming a bank examiner is to get a college degree. Typical majors for this field include accounting, economics, business administration, commercial or banking law, or other business-related subjects. Once you have graduated from college, you may choose to work immediately for a regulatory agency or you may gain applied business experience by working, for example, for a financial institution. Either option is acceptable, though more and more regulatory agencies are actively recruiting candidates who have some business experience. Another possibility is to complete your education while working at the same time through such programs as the OCC's Bank Examiner Cooperative Education Program. Remember, though, that whatever route you pick, you won't become a full-fledged bank examiner overnight. Those who begin their careers working for a regulatory agency generally start as *assistant* or *associate examiners*. If you enter the field after gaining business experience, you may start at a higher level position, but it will still take some time and training to become a bank examiner.

Regulatory agencies provide rigorous training for their bank examiners. Assistant bank examiners must take a series of courses and tests during their first several years as employees of a regulatory agency. They also gain on-the-job experience by working on examination teams. To become a bank examiner, you will need five or more years of experience in auditing or examining financial institutions. In addition, candidates with the best potential for advancement have experience with evaluating computer risk management in financial institutions. That is, they have a great deal of knowledge about assessing the security and flexibility of a financial institution's computer system.

Certification or Licensing

Bank examiners must be commissioned (approved) to examine banks only by a state or federal regulator before they can function as full-fledged examiners. This process typically takes five years. The Bank Administration Institute, an organization for financial professionals, also offers a number of courses that can help individuals prepare for careers as examiners.

Other Requirements

Successful bank examiners are committed to lifelong learning. Even after you have reached the position of bank examiner, it will be important for you to stay on top of new computer developments, laws and regulations, and changes in the field. Also, you should be able to work well with others since you will be working with teams of examiners as well as interacting with professionals at the financial institutions being examined. Be prepared to travel as part of your job; often you will be sent from one financial institution to another to perform examinations. Finally, if you enjoy detailed and analytical work with numbers, this may be the field for you.

Exploring

A good way to learn more about this field is by conducting informational interviews with various banking professionals. You also should read all the literature banks produce in order to learn about different types of accounts and saving mechanisms.

College students should seek part-time jobs or internships within banks. Because bank examiners must be familiar with banking operations from the ground up, one of the best places for a college student to gain experience is by working as a teller in a bank.

Employers

Almost all bank examiners are employees of federal or state governing agencies. They work for the OCC, the Federal Reserve System, the Office of Thrift Supervision, the Federal Deposit Insurance Corporation, and many other federal and state agencies.

Starting Out

College graduates can enter this field via a number of avenues. The Office of Personnel Management (OPM) is the federal government's human resources department. The OPM maintains a list of job listings and also can provide information about requirements, benefits, and salaries.

Individuals also should attempt to contact agencies directly. Most federal regulatory agencies, and many state agencies, maintain job hotlines and Web pages. If possible, job seekers should contact senior officials directly.

The *U.S. Government Manual*, which can be found in most libraries or ordered directly from the Government Printing Office, offers a comprehensive listing of senior managers within all government agencies and departments.

A number of private newsletters, including *Federal Career Opportunities, Federal Jobs Digest*, and *Federal Employee's News Digest*, also list federal job openings.

Advancement

Individuals usually enter this field as assistant examiners and, over the course of four to five years, progress to *commissioned examiners.* Commissioned examiners might be given responsibility for several small banks. As the examiner gains experience and establishes a reputation for integrity, insight, and thoroughness, he or she may be given responsibility for larger banks and larger teams of examiners. Examiners who handle larger banks also tend to earn more money.

After many years, an examiner may be offered a supervisory position. Supervisors usually stay in one office and are responsible for managing a large number of examiners who are working in the field.

Examiners also advance by moving to agencies that offer higher salary scales. Still others leave the profession entirely and put their skills to work as banking consultants. Because examiners study so many different banks, of varying degrees of soundness and efficiency, they can become highly successful, sought-after consultants.

Earnings

Most federal jobs are ranked according to a General Schedule (GS) rating. This rating corresponds to a specific salary range. Positions that require a college education automatically start out at GS-5, which in 2000 corresponds to a range of $21,370 to $27,778. Each level includes ten steps. The amount of increase between each step is uniform. The amount of increase between each step within GS-5, for example is $712. The amount of increase between each step within GS-6 is $794. With experience, examiners for federal agencies can rise quickly to higher GS levels.

Some regulatory organizations, such as the OCC and the Federal Reserve, have developed their own salary scales. Salaries vary depending on factors such as position, experience, and even location, with those living in large cities paid at a higher rate to compensate for cost of living. The OCC Web site, for example, listed a position for an assistant national bank examiner for its offices in the central United States with a beginning salary of $33,800 in the summer of 2000. A national bank examiner's position in the western United States was advertised with a beginning salary of $65,680 at that same time. And an examiner position in Washington, DC, was advertised with the top salary range of $108,138.

"Most experienced examiners earn about $60,000," notes Seifried, "but it depends largely on where they want to end up. Supervisors can earn substantially more than that, but they also have additional responsibilities and pressures."

Most state and federal employees receive excellent benefits, such as health insurance, dental and vision coverage, life insurance, retirement packages, savings plans, sick leave, paid holidays, disability insurance, and child care allowance. The benefits for government employees tend to be extremely competitive and difficult to match in the private sector.

Work Environment

A bank examiner is a nomadic creature, spending several weeks or months in each location before moving on. Bank examiners often work closely with teams of up to 30 or 40 other examiners who also are separated from their family and friends. Most examination teams develop a strong sense of camaraderie that sustains them during the weeks they must live out of hotels. To compensate for the travel, many regulatory agencies offer examiners an extra day off every other week. Examiners who work in these agencies work 9 business days and take the tenth day off.

Bank examiners work in temporary offices, surrounded by professionals who may harbor ambiguous feelings about being examined. The work, however, can be interesting and rewarding.

"It can be a great job," says Seifried. "I was with the OCC for more than 25 years and I spent 23 of those years in the field. I loved that part of it. When you're in the field, you are surrounded by knowledgeable people who have a strong interest in getting problems resolved. You also have a lot of interesting conversations."

Outlook

The U.S. Department of Labor predicts job growth to be about as fast as the average through 2008 for inspectors and compliance officers, which includes bank examiners. However, the banking industry is undergoing tremendous consolidation. As more and more banks merge, fewer examiners may be needed at the state and federal levels. While there may be fewer new positions in this job, those who do enter the field can expect considerable job security. Employment in this field is usually not affected by general economic fluctuations. In addition, job openings will result from the need to replace those who retire or leave for other positions.

For More Information

BAI is an organization for financial professionals that offers newsletters about the financial industry as well as courses in bank auditing and examining.

Bank Administration Institute (BAI)
One North Franklin, Suite 1000
Chicago, IL 60606-3421
Email: info@bai.org
Web: http://www.bai.org

The Federal Reserve System supervises and regulates banking, maintains the stability of the financial system, and provides certain financial services.

Board of Governors of the Federal Reserve System
20th and Constitution Avenue, NW
Washington, DC 20551
Web: http://www.federalreserve.gov/

The Federal Deposit Insurance Corporation can offer information about policies, regulations, and career opportunities.

Federal Deposit Insurance Corporation
500 West Monroe Street, Suite 3300
Chicago, IL 60661
Web: http://www.fdic.gov

Bookkeeping and Accounting Clerks

Overview

Bookkeeping and accounting clerks record financial transactions for government, business, and other organizations. They compute, classify, record, and verify numerical data in order to develop and maintain accurate financial records. There are over two million bookkeeping and accounting clerks employed in the United States.

History

The history of bookkeeping developed along with the growth of business and industrial enterprise. The first known records of bookkeeping date back to 2600 BC, when the Babylonians used pointed sticks to mark accounts on clay slabs. By 3000 BC, Middle Eastern and Egyptian cultures employed a system of numbers to record merchants' transactions of the grain and farm products that were distributed from storage warehouses. The growth of intricate trade systems brought about the necessity for bookkeeping systems.

Sometime after the start of the 13th century, the decimal numeration system was introduced in Europe, simplifying bookkeeping record systems. The merchants of Venice—one of the busiest trading centers in the world at that time—are credited with the invention of the double entry bookkeeping method that is widely used today.

As industry in the United States expands and grows more complex, simpler and quicker bookkeeping methods and procedures have evolved. Technological developments include bookkeeping machines, computer hardware and software, and electronic data-processing.

The Job

Bookkeeping workers keep systematic records and current accounts of financial transactions for businesses, institutions, industries, charities, and other organizations. The bookkeeping records of a firm or business are a vital part of its operational procedures because these records reflect the assets and the liabilities, as well as the profits and losses, of the operation.

Bookkeepers record these business transactions daily in spreadsheets on computer databases, and accounting clerks often input the information. The practice of posting accounting records directly onto ledger sheets, in journals, or on other types of written accounting forms is decreasing as computerized recordkeeping becomes more widespread. In small businesses, bookkeepers sort and record all the sales slips, bills, check stubs, inventory lists, and requisition lists. They compile figures for cash receipts, accounts payable and receivable, and profits and losses.

Accounting clerks handle the clerical accounting work; they enter and verify transaction data and compute and record various charges. They may also monitor loans and accounts payable and receivable. More advanced clerks may reconcile billing vouchers, while senior workers review invoices and statements.

Accountants set up bookkeeping systems and use bookkeepers' balance sheets to prepare periodic summary statements of financial transactions. Management relies heavily on these bookkeeping records to interpret the organization's overall performance and uses them to make important business decisions. The records are also necessary to file income tax reports and prepare quarterly reports for stockholders.

Bookkeeping and accounting clerks work in retail and wholesale businesses, manufacturing firms, hospitals, schools, charities, and other types of institutional agencies. Many clerks are classified as financial institution bookkeeping and accounting clerks, insurance firm bookkeeping and accounting clerks, hotel bookkeeping and accounting clerks, and railroad bookkeeping and accounting clerks.

General bookkeepers and *general-ledger bookkeepers* are usually employed in smaller business operations. They may perform all the analysis, maintain the financial records, and complete any other tasks that are involved in keeping a full set of bookkeeping records. These employees may have other general office duties, such as mailing statements, answering telephone calls, and filing materials. Audit clerks verify figures and may be responsible for sending them on to an audit clerk supervisor.

In large companies, an accountant may supervise a department of bookkeepers who perform more specialized work. *Billing and rate clerks* and *fixed capital clerks* may post items in accounts payable or receivable ledgers, make out bills and invoices, or verify the company's rates for certain products and services. *Account information clerks* prepare reports, compile payroll lists and deductions, write company checks, and compute federal tax reports or personnel profit shares. Large companies may employ workers to organize, record, and compute many other types of financial information.

In large business organizations, bookkeepers and accountants may be classified by grades, such as Bookkeeper I or II. The job classification determines their responsibilities.

Requirements

High School

Employers require bookkeepers to have at least a high school diploma and look for people with backgrounds in business mathematics, business writing, typing, and computer training. Students should pay particular attention to developing sound English and communication skills along with mathematical abilities.

Postsecondary Training

Some employers prefer people who have completed a junior college curriculum or those who have attended a post-high school business training program. In many instances, employers offer on-the-job training for various types of entry-level positions. In some areas, work-study programs are available in which schools, in cooperation with businesses, offer part-time, practical on-the-job training combined with academic study. These programs often help students find immediate employment in similar work after graduation. Local business schools may also offer evening courses.

Other Requirements

Bookkeepers need strong mathematical skills and organizational abilities, and they have to be able to concentrate on detailed work. The work is quite sedentary and often tedious, and bookkeepers should not mind long hours behind a desk. They should be methodical, accurate, and orderly and enjoy working on detailed tasks. Employers look for honest, discreet, and trustworthy individuals when placing their business in someone else's hands.

Bookkeeping and accounting clerks may be required to have union membership at some places of business. Larger unions include the Office and Professional Employees International Union; the International Union of Electronics, Electrical, Salaried, Machine, and Furniture Workers; and the American Federation of State, County, and Municipal Employees. Also, depending on the business, clerks may be represented by the same union as other manufacturing employees.

Exploring

You can gain experience in bookkeeping by participating in work-study programs or by obtaining part-time or summer work in beginning bookkeeping jobs or related office work. Any retail experience dealing with cash management, pricing, or customer service is also valuable.

You can also volunteer to manage the books for extracurricular student groups. Managing income or cash flow for a club or acting as treasurer for student government are excellent ways to gain experience in maintaining financial records.

Other options are visiting local small businesses to observe their work and talking to representatives of schools that offer business training courses.

Employers

Of the more than two million bookkeeping and accounting clerks, roughly 25 percent are employed in the retail and wholesale trade. Many others are employed by organizations that provide educational, health, business, and social services.

Starting Out

High school students may find jobs or establish contacts with businesses that are interested in interviewing graduates through their guidance or placement offices. A work-study program or internship may result in a full-time job offer. Business schools and junior colleges generally provide assistance to their graduates in locating employment.

Applicants may locate job opportunities by applying directly to firms or responding to ads in newspaper classified sections. State employment agencies and private employment bureaus can also assist in the job search process.

Advancement

Bookkeeping workers generally begin their employment by performing routine tasks, such as the simple recording of transactions. Beginners may start as entry-level clerks, cashiers, bookkeeping machine operators, office assistants, or typists. With experience, they may advance to more complex assignments that include computer training in databases and spreadsheets and assume a greater responsibility for the work as a whole.

With experience and education, clerks become department heads or office managers. Further advancement to positions, such as office or division manager, department head, accountant, or auditor is possible with a college degree and years of experience. There is a high turnover rate in this field, which increases the promotion opportunities for employees with ability and initiative.

Earnings

According to the U.S. Department of Labor, bookkeepers and accounting clerks earned a median income of $23,190 a year in 1998. The department also reported that record clerks (which include the position of bookkeeping and accounting clerks) who work for the federal government earned starting salaries of about $18,400 in 1999. Bookkeeping and accounting clerks' earnings are also influenced by such factors as the size of the city where they work and the size and type of business for which they are employed. Those with one or two years of college generally earn higher starting wages. Experienced workers earn an average of $26,000. Top paying jobs average about $30,000 a year.

Employees usually receive six to eight paid holidays yearly and one week of paid vacation after six to twelve months of service. Paid vacations may increase to four weeks or more, depending on length of service and place of employment. Fringe benefits may include health and life insurance, sick leave, and retirement plans.

Work Environment

The majority of office workers, including bookkeeping workers, usually work a 40-hour week, although some employees may work a 35- to 37-hour week. Bookkeeping and accounting clerks usually work in typical office settings. They are more likely to have a cubicle than an office. While the work pace is steady, it can also be routine and repetitive, especially in large companies where the employee is often assigned only one or two specialized job duties.

Attention to numerical details can be physically demanding, and the work can produce eyestrain and nervousness. While bookkeepers usually work with other people and sometimes under close supervision, they can expect to spend most of their day behind a desk; this may seem confining to people who need more variety and stimulation in their work. In addition, the constant attention to detail and the need for accuracy can place considerable responsibility on the worker and cause much stress.

Outlook

Although the growing economy produces a demand for increased accounting services, the automation of office functions will continue to improve overall worker productivity. Fewer people will be needed to do the work, and employment of bookkeeping and accounting clerks is expected to decline through 2008. Excellent computer skills will be vital to securing a job.

Despite lack of growth, there will be numerous replacement job openings since the turnover rate in this occupation is high. Offices are centralizing their operations, setting up one center to manage all accounting needs in a single location. As more companies trim back their workforces, opportunities for temporary work should continue to grow.

For More Information

For information on general accounting careers, contact:

Foundation for Accounting Education
530 Fifth Avenue, 5th Floor
New York, NY 10036-5101
Tel: 800-633-6320

Commodities Brokers

School Subjects
Business
Mathematics

Personal Skills
Communication/ideas
Leadership/management

Work Environment
Primarily indoors
Primarily one location

Minimum Education Level
High school diploma

Salary Range
$22,660 to $48,090
to $1,000,000+

Certification or Licensing
Required by all states

Outlook
Much faster than the average

Overview

Commodities brokers, also known as *futures commission merchants*, act as agents in carrying out purchases and sales of commodities for customers or traders. Commodities are primary goods that are either raw or partially refined. Such goods are produced by farmers, such as corn, wheat, or cattle, or mined from the earth, such as gold, copper, or silver. Brokers, who may work at a brokerage house, on the floor of a commodities exchange, or independently, are paid a fee or commission for acting as the middleman to conduct and complete the trade.

History

In medieval Europe, business was transacted at local market fairs, and commodities, primarily agricultural, were traded at scheduled times and places. As market fairs grew, "fair letters" were set up as a currency representing a future cash settlement for a transaction. With these letters, merchants could travel from one fair to another. This was the precursor to the Japanese system in which landowners used "certificates of receipt" for their rice crops. As the certificates made their way into the economy, the Dojima Rice Market was established and became the first place where traders bought and sold contracts for the future delivery of rice. "Forward contracts" entered the U.S. marketplace in the early 19th century. Farmers, swept up in the boom of industrial growth, transportation, and commerce, began to arrange for the future sale of their crops. Traders entered the market along with the development of these contracts. However, there were no regulations to oversee that the commodity was actually delivered or that it was of an acceptable quality. Furthermore, each transaction was an individual business deal because the terms of each contract were variable. To address these issues, the Chicago Board of Trade was formed in 1848, and by 1865 had set up standards and rules for trading "to arrive" contracts, now known as commodity futures contracts.

The Job

A futures contract is an agreement to deliver a particular commodity, such as wheat, pork bellies, or coffee, at a specific date, time, and place. For example, a farmer might sell his oats before they are sowed (known as "hedging") because he can't predict what kind of price he'll be able to demand later on. If the weather is favorable and crops are good, he'll have competition, which will drive prices down. If there is a flood or drought, oats will be scarce, driving the price up. He wants to ensure fair price for his product to protect his business and limit his risk since he can't predict what will happen.

On the other side of the equation is the user of the oats, perhaps a cereal manufacturer, who purchases these contracts for a delivery of oats at some future date. The third party is the speculator, or trader, who is neither a producer or consumer. Traders enter the market to make a profit by anticipating the direction of the commodity's price. Producers and consumers do not correspond to a one-to-one ratio, and it is the trader who acts as the middleman in the buying and selling of contracts.

Brokers place the trades of speculators who cannot place their own if they are not a member of an exchange. Brokers are paid a fee or commission for acting as the agent in making the sale. There are two broad categories of brokers, though they are becoming less distinct. *Full service brokers* provide considerable research to clients, offer price quotes, give trading advice, and assist the customer in making trading decisions. *Discount brokers* simply fill the orders as directed by clients. Some brokers offer intermediate levels of optional services on a sliding scale of commission, such as market research and strategic advice.

In general, brokers are responsible for taking and carrying out all commodity orders and being available on call to do so; reporting back to the client upon fulfilling the order request; keeping the client abreast of breaking news; maintaining account balances and other financial data; and obtaining market information when needed and informing the client about important changes in the marketplace.

Brokers can work on the floor of a commodity futures exchange—the marketplace where contracts are bought and sold—for a brokerage house, or independently. The exchange houses the trading floor where brokers transact their business in the trading pit. There are 11 domestic exchanges, with the main ones in Chicago, Kansas City, New York, and Minneapolis. A broker or trader must be a member of an exchange, which is a private membership organization. Membership is limited to a specific and small number of individuals who must purchase or rent a seat on the floor, which is quite expensive. Purchasing a seat on the Chicago Exchange, for example, costs $760,000 and also entails a thorough investigation of the applicant's credit standing, financial background, and character. Most brokers, therefore, work for a brokerage house dealing in futures. These may be companies like Merrill Lynch or Dean Witter, which deal in stocks, bonds, commodities, and other investments, or smaller houses such as R.J. O'Brien, which handle only commodities.

Companies can also have a seat on the exchange, and they have their own *floor brokers* in the pit to carry out trades for the brokerage house. Brokers in the company take orders from the public for buying or selling a contract and promptly pass it on to the floor broker in the pit of the exchange. Brokers also have the choice of running their own business. Known as *introducing brokers*, they handle their own clients and trades and use brokerage houses to place their orders. Introducing brokers earn a fee by soliciting business trades, but they don't directly handle the customer's funds.

Requirements

High School

Although there are no formal educational requirments for becoming a broker, a high school and a college degree are strongly recommended. Commodities brokers need to have a wide range of knowledge, covering such areas as economics, world politics, and sometimes even the weather. To begin to develop this broad-base of knowledge, start in high school by taking history, math, science, and business classes. Since commodities brokers are constantly working with people to make a sale, take English classes to enhance your communication skills. In addition to this course work, you might also consider getting a part-time job working in a sales position. Such a job will also give you the chance to hone your communication and sales skills.

Postsecondary Training

The vast majority of brokers have a college degree. While there is no "commodities broker major," you can improve your chances of obtaining a job in this field by studying economics, finance, or business administration while in college. Keep in mind that you should continue to develop your understanding of politics and technologies, so government and computer classes will also be useful.

Brokerage firms look for employees who have sales ability, strong communication skills, and self-confidence. Commodities is often a second career for many people who have demonstrated these qualities in other positions.

Certification or Licensing

To become a commodities broker, it is necessary to pass the National Commodities Futures Examination (the Series 3 exam) to become eligible to satisfy the registration requirements of federal, state, and industry regulatory agencies. The test covers market and trading knowledge, as well as rules and regulations. The test costs $75 and is available through the National Futures Association. The Commodity Education Institute offers week-long courses to prepare for the exam. Brokers must also register with the National Futures Association. Floor brokers, however, are not required to take the exam and are instead put through a rigorous training program at the exchange.

Other Requirements

Brokers must possess a combination of research and money management skills. They need to be attentive to detail and have a knack for analyzing data. Strong communications and sales skills are important as well, as brokers make money by convincing people to let them place their trades. An interest in and awareness of the world around them is also a contributing factor to a broker's success, as commodities are influenced by everything from political decisions and international news to social and fashion trends.

Brokers must also be emotionally stable to work in such a volatile environment. They need to be persistent, aggressive, and comfortable taking risks and dealing with failure. Strong, consistent, and independent judgment is also key. Brokers must be disciplined hard workers, able to comb through reams of market reports and charts to gain a thorough understanding of their particular commodity and the mechanics of the marketplace. They also need to be outspoken and assertive, able to yell out prices loudly and energetically on the trading floor and command attention.

Exploring

Students interested in commodities trading should visit one of the futures exchanges. All of them offer public tours, and you'll get to see up close just how the markets work and the roles of the players involved. All the exchanges offer educational programs and publications, and most have a page on the World Wide Web. (See "For More Information.") The Chicago Mercantile Exchange publishes *The Merc at Work*, the full text of which is also available on the Internet, as well as many other educational handbooks and pamphlets. There are hundreds of industry newsletters and magazines available (such as *Futures Magazine*), and many offer free samples of publications or products. Read what trading advisors have to say and how they say it. Learn their lingo and gain an understanding of the marketplace. If you have any contacts in the industry, arrange to spend a day with a broker. Watch him or her work, and you'll learn how orders are entered, processed, and reported.

Do your own research. Adopt a commodity, chart its prices, test some of your own ideas, and analyze the marketplace. There are also a variety of inexpensive software programs, as well as sites on the Web, that simulate trading.

Finally, consider a job as a runner during the summer before your freshman year in college. Runners transport the order, or "paper," from the phone clerk to the broker in the pit and relay information to and from members on the floor. This is the single best way to get hands-on experience in the industry.

Employers

Commodities brokers work on the floor of a commodity futures exchange, for brokerage houses, or independently.

Starting Out

College graduates can start working with a brokerage house as an associate and begin handling stocks. After several years they can take the certification exam and move into futures. Another option is to start as support staff, either at the exchange or the brokerage house. Sales personnel try to get customers to open accounts, and account executives develop and service customers for the brokerage firm. At the exchange, phone clerks receive incoming orders and communicate the information to the runners. Working in the back as an accountant, money manager, or member of the research staff is also another route. School placement offices may be able to assist graduates in finding jobs with brokerage houses. Applications may also be made directly to brokerage houses themselves.

Many successful brokers and traders began their careers as a runner, and each exchange has its own training program. Though the pay is low, runners learn the business very quickly with a hands-on experience not available in an academic classroom. Contact one of the commodities exchanges for information on becoming a runner.

Advancement

A broker who simply executes trades can advance to become a full-service broker. Through research and analysis and the accumulation of experience and knowledge about the industry, a broker can advance from an order filler and become a commodity trading advisor. A broker can also become a money manager and make all trading decisions for clients.

Within the exchange, a broker can become a floor manager, overseeing the processes of order-taking and information exchange. To make more money, a broker can also begin to place his or her own trades for his or her own private account, though the broker's first responsibility is to the customers.

Earnings

This is an entrepreneurial business. A broker's commission is based on the number of clients he or she recruits, the more they invest, and the amount of money they make. The sky's the limit. In recent years the most successful broker made $25 million. A typical salary for a newly hired employee in a brokerage might average $1,500 per month plus a 30 percent commission on sales. Smaller firms are likely to pay a smaller commission. The U.S. Department of Labor reports that the median annual earnings for securities, commodities, and financial services sales representatives were $48,090 in 1998. The lowest 10 percent earned less than $22,600; the highest 10 percent earned more than $124,800 annually.

Working with the Chicago Board of Trade, the world's leading futures exchange, offers numerous benefits. Employees are eligible for vacation six months after employment and receive three weeks after three years. Employees are also paid for sick days, personal days, and eight holidays. During the summer months various departments offer flex time, allowing employees to take Fridays off by working longer hours during the week. Employees also receive numerous forms of insurance, including medical, life, and disability. Full tuition reimbursement is available as is a company-matched savings plan, a tax-deferred savings plan, and a pension program. Other large exchanges and brokerage houses offer similar combinations of benefits.

Work Environment

The trading floor is noisy and chaotic, as trading is done using an "open outcry" system. Every broker must be an auctioneer, yelling out his own price bids for purchases and sales. The highest bid wins and silences all the others. When a broker's primal scream is not heard, bids and offers can also be communicated with hand signals.

Brokers stand for most of the day, often in the same place, so that traders interested in their commodity can locate them easily. Each broker wears a distinctly colored jacket with a prominent identification badge. The letter on the badge identifies the broker and appears on the paperwork relating to the trade. Members of the exchange and employees of member firms wear red jackets. Some brokers and traders also have uniquely patterned jackets to further increase their visibility in the pit.

Brokers and traders do not have a nine-to-five job. While commodities trading on the exchange generally takes place from 9:00 AM to 1:00 PM, international trading runs from 2:45 PM to 6:50 AM.

In the rough and tumble world of the futures exchange, emotions run high as people often win or lose six-figure amounts within hours. Tension is fierce, the pace is frantic, and angry, verbal, and sometimes physical exchanges are not uncommon.

Outlook

The U.S. Bureau of Labor Statistics predicts much faster than the average growth—about 41 percent—for securities and financial sales representatives through 2008. Two major trends are affecting the future of the commodities industry: international growth and new technology. Though the industry on the whole is small (50,000 firms as compared to the 400,000 firms in securities) and firms are sizing down, the number of exchanges has doubled in the last 10 years, and in 1998 there were 68 exchanges in 28 countries. The United States used to control 90 percent of the world's business, and now accounts for just 45 percent. Opportunities to manage commodities are no longer limited to the United States.

New commodities are also bursting onto the scene. During the 1980s, 186 new futures contracts were introduced. And nearly half of the total volume of trades were a product of these new contracts. Look for new types of commodities to continue to grow along with the move toward globalization, and for brokers to become highly specialized.

New computer and information technology is rapidly influencing and advancing the industry. A growing number of exchanges now use electronic systems to automate trades, and many use them exclusively. Many systems have unique features designed specifically to meet customers' needs. New technology, such as electronic order entry, hookups to overseas exchanges, and night trading, is rapidly evolving, offering brokers new ways to manage risk and provide price information.

For More Information

For information on the industry, the National Commodity Futures Exam, how to become an Associated Person or Introducing Broker, contact:

Center for Futures Education
410 Erie Street
PO Box 309
Grove City, PA 16127
Tel: 724-458-5860
Email: info@thectr.com
Web: http://www.thectr.com/

The Chicago Mercantile Exchange offers a wide variety of materials on commodities careers through its Web site.

Chicago Mercantile Exchange
30 South Wacker Drive
Chicago, IL 60606
Tel: 312-930-1000
Email: edu@cme.com
Web: http://www.cme.com

For information on the National Commodities Futures Examination, contact:

National Futures Association
200 West Madison Street, Suite 1600
Chicago, IL 60606
Tel: 800-621-3570
Web: http://www.nfa.futures.org/

The educational section of the Philadelphia Board of Trade's Web site provides a glossary of terms, suggested reading, and an overview of the financial industry.

Philadelphia Board of Trade
1900 Market Street
Philadelphia, PA 19103-3584
Tel: 215-496-5000
Email: info@phlx.com
Web: http://www.phlx.com

Credit Analysts

Overview

Credit analysts analyze financial information to evaluate the amount of risk involved in lending money to businesses or individuals. They contact banks, credit associations, and others to obtain credit information and prepare a written report of findings used to recommend credit limits. There are approximately 42,000 credit analysts employed in the United States.

History

Only 50 or 75 years ago, lending money was based mainly on a person's reputation. Money was lent after a borrower talked with friends and business acquaintances. Now, of course, much more financial background information is demanded. The use of credit cards and other forms of borrowing has skyrocketed in the last several years and today only accepted forms of accounting are used to determine if a loan applicant is a good risk. As business and financial institutions have grown more complex, the demand for professional credit analysis has also expanded.

The Job

Credit analysts typically concentrate on one of two different areas. *Commercial and business analysts* evaluate risks in business loans; *consumer credit analysts* evaluate personal loan risks. In both cases an analyst studies financial documents such as a statement of assets and liabilities submitted by the person or company seeking the loan and consults with banks and other financial institutions that have previous financial relationships with the applicant. Credit analysts prepare, analyze, and approve loan requests, and help borrowers fill out applications.

The scope of work involved in a credit check depends in large part on the size and type of the loan requested. A background check on a $3,000 car loan, for example, is much less detailed than on a $400,000 commercial improvement loan for an expanding business. In both cases, financial statements and applicants will be checked by the credit analyst, but the larger loan will entail a much closer look at economic trends to determine if there is a market for the product being produced and the likelihood of the business failing. Because of these responsibilities, many credit analysts work solely with commercial loans.

In studying a commercial loan application, a credit analyst is interested in determining if the business or corporation is well managed and financially secure and if the existing economic climate is favorable for the operation's success. To do this, a credit analyst examines balance sheets and operating statements to determine the assets and liabilities of a company, its net sales, and its profits or losses. An analyst must be familiar with accounting and bookkeeping methods to ensure that the applicant company is operating under accepted accounting principles. A background check of the applicant company's leading officials is also done to determine if they personally have any outstanding loans. An on-site visit by the analyst may also be necessary to compare how the company's operations stack up against its competitors.

Analyzing economic trends to determine market conditions is another responsibility of the credit analyst. To do this, the credit analyst computes dozens of ratios to show how successful the company is in relation to similar businesses. Profit-and-loss statements, collection procedures, and a host of other factors are analyzed. This ratio analysis can also be used to measure how successful a particular industry is likely to be, given existing market considerations. Computer programs are used to highlight economic trends and interpret other important data.

The credit analyst always provides a findings report to bank executives. This report includes a complete financial history of the applicant and usually concludes with a recommendation on the loan amount, if any, that should be advanced.

Requirements

High School

If you are interested in this career, take courses in mathematics, economics, business, and accounting in high school. You should also take English courses to develop sound oral and written language skills. Computer courses will help you to become computer literate, learn software programs, understand their applications to particular fields, and gain familiarity with accessing electronic information.

Postsecondary Training

Most credit analysts have a bachelor's degree in accounting, finance, or business administration, although some have only a high school diploma or a two-year degree. Higher education, though, is directly associated with higher salaries in the field. College course work should include business management, economics, statistics, and accounting. In addition, keep honing your computer skills. Some credit analysts go on to receive a master's in business administration (MBA) or a master's in another related field.

Other Requirements

Credit analysts should have an aptitude for mathematics and be adept at organizing, assessing, and reporting data. They must be able to analyze complex problems and devise resourceful solutions. Credit analysts also need strong interpersonal skills. They must be able to interview loan applicants and communicate effectively, establish solid working relationships with customers as well as coworkers, and clearly relate the results of their work.

Exploring

For information on the credit management industry, survey newsgroups and Web pages on the Internet that are related to this field. The Credit Management Information and Support site, http://www.creditworthy.com, offers informative interviews with people in the field and advice for breaking into the business. This site also has a section that describes educational resources and offers an online course in the basics of business credit. The National Association of Credit Management Web site, http://www.nacm.org, has links to other industry sites.

Consider a position as treasurer for student council or other student-run organizations. This will introduce you to the responsibilities associated with managing money. Or explore a part-time job as a bank clerk, teller, or customer service representative that will familiarize you with banking procedures. This is also a good way to network with professionals in the banking field. Various clubs and organizations may have opportunities for volunteers to develop experience working with budgets and financial statements. Local institutions and small or single-owner businesses may welcome students interested in learning more about financial operations.

Employers

Credit analysts are employed by banks, credit unions, credit agencies, business credit institutions, credit bureaus, corporations, and loan companies. They are also employed by hotels, hospitals, and department stores.

Starting Out

Although some people enter the field with a high school or two-year degree, most entry-level positions go to college graduates with degrees in fields such as accounting, finance, economics, and business administration. Credit analysts receive much of their formal training and learn specific procedures and requirements on the job. Many employees also rise through the ranks via other positions such as teller or customer service representative prior to becoming a credit analyst. Newspaper want ads, school placement services, and direct application to specific employers are all ways of tracking down that first job.

Advancement

Credit analysts generally advance to supervisory positions. However, promotion and salary potential are limited, and many employees often choose to leave a company for better-paying positions elsewhere. After three to five years of credit work, a skilled credit analyst can expect a promotion to *credit manager* and ultimately *chief credit executive*. Responsibilities grow to include training other credit personnel, coordinating the credit department with other internal operations, and managing relations with customers and financial institutions.

Earnings

Salaries of credit analysts depend on the individual's experience and education. The size of the financial institution is also a determining factor: large banks tend to pay more than smaller operations. Salaries also increase with the number of years in the field and with a particular company. According to a 1999 survey by Romac International (a staffing and recruiting firm), entry-level credit analysts averaged an annual salary of $27,800. Credit analysts in management positions averaged $52,100. The U.S. Department of Labor reported an average yearly income of $33,020 for credit analysts in 1998. A survey by the Credit Research Foundation also shows that employees with advanced degrees earn the highest incomes.

As an added perk, many banks offer their credit analysts free checking privileges and lower interest rates on personal loans. Other benefits include health insurance, sick and vacation pay, and retirement plans.

Work Environment

Most credit analysts work in typical corporate office settings that are well lighted and air-conditioned in the summertime. Credit analysts can expect to work a 40-hour week, but they may have to put in overtime if a project has a tight deadline. A commercial credit analyst may have to travel to the business or corporation that is seeking a loan in order to prepare the agreement. Credit analysts can expect heavy caseloads. Respondents to the annual survey of the National Association of Credit Management reported handling 250 to 2,000 active accounts per year.

A credit analyst should be able to spend long hours behind a desk quietly reading and analyzing financial reports. Attention to detail is critical. Credit analysts can expect to work in high-pressure situations, with loans of millions of dollars dependent on their analysis.

Outlook

There are approximately 42,000 credit analysts employed in the United States. As the field of cash management grows along with the economy and the population, banks and other financial institutions will need more credit analysts. According to the U.S. Department of Labor, job prospects are expected to grow about as fast as the average through 2008. Credit analysts are crucial to the success and profitability of banks, and the number, variety, and complexity of credit applications are on the rise. Banks hire about half of all credit analysts, so opportunities should be best in areas with the largest and greatest number of banks.

Credit analysts are particularly busy when interest rates drop and applications surge. Job security is influenced by the local economy and business climate. However, loans are a major source of income for banks, and credit officers are less likely to lose their jobs in an economic downturn.

Information technology is affecting the field of credit analysis as public financial information, as well as economic and market research, becomes more accessible via the Internet. Credit professionals now have a broader range of data available upon which to base decisions.

For More Information

The ABA offers general banking industry information.

American Bankers Association (ABA)
1120 Connecticut Avenue, NW
Washington, DC 20036
Tel: 800-226-5377
Web: http://www.aba.com/

The Institute offers a wide variety of publications and continuing education and training formats for financial institution workers.

Bank Administration Institute
One North Franklin, Suite 1000
Chicago, IL 60606-3421
Tel: 800-224-9889
Email: info@bai.org
Web: http://www.bai.org

This educational and research organization has information on the industry.

Credit Research Foundation
8840 Columbia 100 Parkway
Columbia, MD 21045
Tel: 410-740-5499
Email: crf_info@crfonline.org
Web: http://www.crfonline.org

For information on certification, continuing education, and general information on the banking and credit industry, contact:

National Association of Credit Management
8840 Columbia 100 Parkway
Columbia, MD 21045-2158
Tel: 410-740-5560
Email: nacm_info@nacm.org
Web: http://www.nacm.org

Financial Institution Clerks and Related Workers

School Subjects
Business
Mathematics

Personal Skills
Following instructions
Mechanical/manipulative

Work Environment
Primarily indoors
Primarily one location

Minimum Education Level
High school diploma

Salary Range
$16,220 to $22,580 to $29,250

Certification or Licensing
None available

Outlook
About as fast as the average

Overview

Financial institution clerks and related workers perform many tasks in banks and other savings institutions. Job duties usually vary with the size of the bank. In small banks, a clerk or related worker may perform a combination of tasks, while in larger banks an employee may be assigned to one specialized duty. All banking activities are concerned with the safekeeping, exchange, record keeping, and credit use of money.

History

The profession of banking is nearly as old as civilization itself. Early literature makes reference to "money-lenders" and "money-changers" as ancient writers and travelers describe how they bought money in other countries by trading coins from their own homelands.

The term banking is derived from the Italian banco, meaning bench. Since the times of the Roman Empire, Italy has been an important trading and shipping nation. In medieval times, bankers set up benches on the streets and from these conducted their business of trading currencies and accepting precious metals and jewels for safekeeping. They also lent money at interest to finance the new ventures of shipping merchants and other businesses. Italian cities eventually established permanent banks, and this practice gradually spread north throughout Europe. During the 17th century important banking developments took place in England, which by that time had become a major trading nation. In 1694, the Bank of England was founded in London.

In the United States the Continental Congress chartered the Bank of North America in 1782 in Philadelphia. The first state bank was chartered in Boston in 1784 as the Bank of Massachusetts. Although the development of banking in the United States has experienced periods of slow growth and numerous failures throughout history, Congress and the federal government have done a great deal to make the nation's banking system safer and more effective.

Today, banking, like many other professions, has turned to the use of automation, mechanization, computers, telecommunications, and many modern methods of bookkeeping and record systems. For all the modern banking conveniences that Americans enjoy today, banks and savings institutions employ thousands of workers so that they can offer these services.

The Job

In the back offices of banks and other institutions, financial institution clerks and related workers perform the work that keeps depositors' money safe, the bank's investments healthy, and government regulations satisfied. All such workers assist in processing the vast amounts of paperwork that a bank generates. This paperwork may consist of deposit slips, checks, financial statements to customers, correspondence, record transactions, or reports for internal and external use. Depending on their job responsibilities, clerks may prepare, collect, send, index, or file these documents. In addition, they may talk with customers and other banks, take telephone calls, and perform other general office duties.

The range of tasks an employee performs depends on the size of the financial institution. Duties may be more generalized in smaller facilities and very specialized at larger institutions. The nature of the bank's business and the array of services it offers may also determine a clerk's duties. Services may differ somewhat in a commercial bank from those in a savings bank, trust company, credit union, or savings and loan. In the past banks generally lent money to businesses while savings and loan and credit unions lent to individuals, but these differences are slowly disappearing over time.

Collection clerks process checks, coupons, and drafts that customers present to the financial institution for special handling. *Commodity-loan clerks* keep track of commodities (usually farm products) used as collateral by the foreign departments of large banks.

Banks employ *bookkeepers* to keep track of countless types of financial and administrative information. *Bookkeeping clerks* file checks, alphabetize paperwork to assist senior bookkeepers, and sort and list various other kinds of material.

Proof machine operators handle a machine which, in one single operation, can sort checks and other papers, add their amounts, and record totals. *Transit clerks* sort and list checks and drafts on other banks and prepare them for mailing back to those banks. *Statement clerks* send customers their account statements listing the withdrawals and deposits they have made. *Bookkeeping machine operators* maintain records of the various deposits, checks, and other items that are credited to or charged against customer accounts. Often they cancel checks and file them, provide customers with information about account balances, and prepare customers' statements for mailing.

Messengers deliver checks, drafts, letters, and other business papers to other financial institutions, business firms, and local and federal government agencies. Messengers who work only within the bank are often known as *pages*. *Trust-mail clerks* keep track of mail in trust departments.

Other clerks—*collateral-and-safekeeping clerks*, *reserves clerks*, and *interest clerks*—collect and record information about collateral, reserves, and interest rates and payments. *Letter-of-credit clerks* keep track of letters of credit for export and import purposes. *Wire-transfer clerks* operate machines that direct the transfer of funds from one account to another.

Many banks now use computers to perform the routine tasks that workers formerly did by hand. To operate these new machines, banks employ computer operators, tabulating machine operators, microfilming machine operators, and electronic reader-sorter operators. *Encoder operators* run machines that print information on checks and other papers in magnetic ink so that machines can read them. *Control clerks* keep track of all the data and paperwork transacted through the electronic data-processing divisions.

Almost all businesses and industries use banking services of one form or another. People employed in banking are usually exposed to a great deal of knowledge of how the general world of business operates and how the stock market operates and influences banking. Banks are usually pleasant, low-stress places to work and have very up-to-date equipment and business machines. People who work in banking are usually people of good character and reputation who enjoy detailed work.

Requirements

High School

Most banks today prefer to hire individuals who have completed high school. If you take courses in computers, bookkeeping, shorthand, typing, business arithmetic, and business machines while in high school, you may have an advantage when applying for a job. Some banks are interested in hiring college graduates (or those who have completed at least two years of college training) who can eventually move into managerial positions. Exchange clerks may be expected to know foreign languages.

Other Requirements

Because the work involves many details, a prime requirement for all bank employees is accuracy. Even the slightest error can cause untold extra hours of work and inconvenience or even monetary loss. A pleasing and congenial personality and the ability to get along well with fellow workers are also necessary in this employment. Often an employee will be required to work closely with other employees or with the public.

The physical requirements of the work are not very demanding. Applicants for jobs are expected to be neat, clean, and appropriately dressed for business.

Banks occasionally require lie detector tests of applicants, as well as fingerprint and background investigations if the job requires handling currency and finances. Those employees handling money may have to qualify for a personal bond. Some banks now require pre-employment drug testing, and random testing for drugs while under employment is becoming more typical.

Although integrity and honesty are important traits for an employee in any type of work, they are absolutely necessary for those persons employed in banks and other financial institutions where large sums of money are handled every day. Workers must also exhibit sound judgment and intelligence in their job performance.

Exploring

You can explore this field further by visiting local financial institutions and talking with the directors of personnel or with people who work in these jobs. Sometimes banks offer part-time employment to young people who feel they have a definite interest in pursuing a career in banking or those with business and clerical skills. Other types of part-time employment—where employees learn basic business skills—may also be valuable training for those planning to enter these occupations.

Employers

Financial institution clerks and related workers are employed by commercial banks and other depository institutions and by mortgage banks and other nondepository institutions.

Starting Out

Private and state employment agencies frequently list available positions for financial institution clerks and related workers. Newspaper help wanted advertisements carry listings for such employees. Some large financial institutions visit schools and colleges to recruit qualified applicants to fill positions on their staff.

If you are interested in a job as a financial institution clerk, try contacting the director of personnel at a bank or other institution to see if any positions are available. If any jobs are open, you may be asked to come in and fill out an application. It is very important, however, to arrange the appointment first by telephone or mail because drop-in visits are disruptive and seldom welcome.

If you know someone who is willing to give you a personal introduction to the director of personnel or to the officers of a bank, you may find that this will help you secure employment. Personal and business references can be important to bank employers when they hire new personnel.

Many financial institution clerks begin their employment as trainees in certain types of work, such as business machine operation or general or specialized clerical duties. Employees may start out as file clerks, transit clerks, or bookkeeping clerks and in some cases as pages or messengers. In general, beginning jobs are determined by the size of the institution and the nature of its operations. In banking work, employees are sometimes trained in related job tasks so that they might be promoted later.

Advancement

Financial institution clerks who perform their jobs well may receive promotions to low-level supervisory positions or advance to positions as tellers or credit analysts. After proving themselves in these positions, they may be promoted to senior supervisory positions. Advancement to an officer position at a bank, however, is usually open only to those employees with college degrees.

Financial institution clerks may receive promotions as they gain job experience and pursue specialized educational training. The Bank Administration Institute, the American Institute of Banking (a division of the American Banking Association), and the Institute of Financial Education offer courses in various banking topics that can help employees show their initiative, learn new skills, and prepare for promotions.

In some cases, financial institution clerks may change jobs or move to larger or different types of banks. Increases in salary or job status may be gained in this way. Other factors that influence promotional opportunities are length of service, extent of educational or specialized training, and job performance.

Earnings

The earnings of financial institution clerks and related workers vary by the specific duties, size and type of institution, and area of the country. According to a salary guide by Robert Half International Inc., accounting clerks at large institutions had an annual salary range of $25,000 to $29,250 in 2000. At small institutions this range was from $22,250 to $26,250. The U.S. Department of Labor reported that in 1998 loan clerks had median yearly earnings of approximately $22,580. The department also reported bookkeeping, accounting, and auditing clerks to have a median annual income of $23,190 in 1998. That same year general office clerks had a median yearly income of $19,580, while statement clerks had a median income of $18,640. In 1997 messengers working for commercial banks had a median hourly wage of $7.80 according to the U.S. Department of Labor. This hourly wage translated into a yearly income of about $16,220 for full-time work.

Financial institution clerks and related workers may receive up to 12 paid holidays a year, depending on their locale. A two-week paid vacation is common after one year of service and can increase to three weeks after 10 or 15 years of service. Fringe benefits usually include group life and health insurance, hospitalization, and jointly financed retirement plans.

Work Environment

Most financial institution workers work a 40-hour week. Bank clerks and accounting department employees may have to work overtime at least once a week and often at the close of each month's banking operations to process important paperwork. Check processing workers who are employed in large financial institutions may work late evening or night shifts. Those employees engaged in computer operations may also work evening or night shifts because this equipment is usually run around the clock. Pay for overtime work is usually straight compensation.

Banks and other depository institutions are usually air-conditioned, pleasantly decorated, and comfortably furnished. Financial institutions have excellent alarm systems and many built-in features that offer protection to workers and facilities. The job duties are not strenuous. In many tasks, very little physical movement is required. The work performed is usually of a very repetitive nature, and the duties are very similar from day to day. Most of the work is paperwork, computer entry, data processing, and other mechanical processes and does not frequently involve customer or client contact.

Individuals must be able to work closely with each other, sometimes on joint tasks, as well as under supervision.

Outlook

The U.S. Department of Labor predicts growth for these positions to be about as fast as the average through 2008. Turnover rates in these jobs are fairly high as employees tire of the repetitive nature of the work, move on to higher-level positions, or leave the workforce. In addition, financial institutions need to employ a large number of people to function properly. Because of these factors, thousands of job opportunities for bank clerks and related workers can be anticipated during the coming years.

As urban areas continue to expand, many banks, trust companies, and savings and loan associations are opening branch operations to bring their services to new customers. This expansion may increase the demand for clerks and related workers. However, closings, mergers, and consolidations of a number of financial institutions makes job opportunities harder to predict in some areas of the country.

It seems likely that the increasing use of computers and electronic data processing methods will decrease the need for some employees such as check sorters, index filers, and bookkeeping machine operators. Financial institutions now face the problem of moving their displaced workers into other jobs through on-the-job training or educating employees in the operation of electronic data processing and computers.

For More Information

For general information about the banking industry and education available through the American Institute of Banking, contact:

American Bankers Association
1120 Connecticut Avenue, NW
Washington, DC 20036
Tel: 800-226-5377
Web: http://www.aba.com/

The Bank Administration Institute has information on continuing education and seminars in banking.

Bank Administration Institute
One North Franklin, Suite 1000
Chicago, IL 60606-3421
Tel: 800-224-9889
Email: info@bai.org
Web: http://www.bai.org

The Institute, which joined forces with BAI in 1999, offers a wide variety of publications and continuing education and training formats for financial institution clerks and related workers.

The Institute of Financial Education
55 West Monroe, Suite 2800
Chicago, IL 60603-5014
Tel: 800-946-0488
Web: http://www.bai.org/ife

Financial Institution Officers and Managers

Business Mathematics	School Subjects
Communication/ideas Leadership/management	Personal Skills
Primarily indoors Primarily one location	Work Environment
Bachelor's degree	Minimum Education Level
$27,680 to $45,800 to $118,950+	Salary Range
Recommended	Certification or Licensing
About as fast as the average	Outlook

Overview

Financial institution officers and managers oversee the activities of banks and personal credit institutions such as credit unions and finance companies. These establishments serve business, government, and individuals. They lend money, maintain savings, enable people and businesses to write checks for goods and services, rent safe-deposit boxes for storing valuables, manage trust funds, advise clients on investments and business affairs, issue credit cards and traveler's checks, and take payments for gas and electric bills. There are approximately 693,000 financial managers, which includes those working outside of financial institutions, employed in the United States.

History

The modern concept of bank notes, or currency, developed in the 17th century. Goldsmiths in London began to issue paper receipts for gold and other valuables that were deposited in their warehouses. The paper money we use today is a modern version of these 17th-century receipts.

The first bank in the United States, Bank of North America, was chartered by the Continental Congress in 1781. By the early 1900s, banks had become so numerous that federal control of banks was needed. The Federal Deposit System, as we know it today, is the result of the efforts to coordinate the activities of the many banks throughout the nation. As banks have grown in numbers, so have their services. They have even changed some of our ideas about money. For example, banks have simplified the problem of carrying around and exchanging large sums of money. Today we use checks. More than 90 percent of all business today is conducted by the use of checks. The number of banks and other financial institutions has grown extensively within the past 25 years, creating many positions for people to conduct their services.

The Job

Financial institutions include commercial banks, which provide full banking service for business, government, and individuals; investment banks, which offer their clients financial counseling and brokering; Federal Reserve Banks, whose customers are affiliated banks in their districts; or other organizations such as credit unions and finance companies.

These institutions employ many officers and managers whose duties vary depending on the type and size of the firm as well as on their own area of responsibility within it. All financial institutions operate under the direction of a president, who is guided by policies set by the board of directors. Vice presidents are department heads who are sometimes also responsible for certain key clients. Controllers handle bank funds, properties, and equipment. Large institutions may also have treasurers, loan officers, and officers in charge of departments such as trust, credit, and investment. A number of these positions are described in more detail in the following paragraphs.

The *financial institution president* directs the overall activities of the bank or consumer credit organization, making sure that its objectives are achieved without violating government regulations or overlooking any legal requirements. The officers are responsible for earning as much of a return as possible on the institution's investments within the restrictions demanded by government and sound business practices. They help set policies pertaining to investments, loans, interest, and reserves. They coordinate the activities of the various divisions and delegate authority to subordinate officers, who administer the operation of their own areas of responsibility. Financial institution presidents study financial reports and other data to keep up with changes in the economy that may affect their firm's policies.

The *vice president* coordinates many of the operations of the institution. This person is responsible for the activities of a regional bank office, branch bank, and often an administrative bank division or department. As designated by the board of directors, the vice president supervises programs such as installment loan, foreign trade, customer service, trust, and investment. The vice president also prepares studies for management and planning, like workload and budget estimates and activity and analysis reports.

The *administrative secretary* usually writes directions for supervisory workers that outline and explain policy. The administrative secretary acts, in effect, as an intermediary between minor supervisory workers and the executive officers.

The *financial institution treasurer* directs the bank's monetary programs, transactions, and security measures in accordance with banking principles and legislation. Treasurers coordinate program activity and evaluate operating practices to ensure efficient operations. They oversee receipt, disbursement, and expenditure of money and sign documents approving or affecting monetary transactions. They direct the safekeeping and control of assets and securities and maintain specified legal cash reserves. They review financial and operating statements and present reports and recommendations to bank officials or board committees.

Controllers authorize and control the use of funds kept by the treasurer. They also supervise the maintenance of accounts and records, and analyze these records so that the directors or other bank officials will know how much the bank is spending for salaries, operating expenses, and other expenses. Controllers often formulate financial policies.

The *financial institution manager* establishes and maintains relationships with the community. This person's responsibility is to supervise accounting and reporting functions and to establish operating policies and procedures. The manager directs several activities within the bank. The assets, records, collateral, and securities held by the financial institution are in the manager's custody. Managers approve credit and commercial, real estate, and consumer loans, and direct personnel in trust activities.

The *loan officer* and the *credit and collection manager* both deal with customers who are seeking or have obtained loans or credit. The loan officer specializes in examining and evaluating applications for lines of credit, installment credit, or commercial, real estate, and consumer loans and has the authority to approve them within a specified limit or recommend their approval to the loan committee. To determine the feasibility of granting a loan request, the officer analyzes the applicant's financial status, credit, and property evaluation. The job may also include handling foreclosure proceedings. Depending on training and experience, officers may analyze potential loan markets to develop prospects for loans. They negotiate the terms of transaction and draw up the requisite documents to buy and sell contracts, loans, or real estate. Credit and collection managers make up collection notices for customers who already have credit. When the bank has difficulty collecting accounts or receives a worthless check, credit and collection managers take steps to correct the situation. Managers must keep records of all credit and collection transactions.

Loan counselors study the records of the account when payments on a loan are overdue and contact the borrower to discuss payment of the loan. They may analyze the borrower's financial problems and make new arrangements for repayment of the loan. If a loan account is uncollectible, they prepare a report for the bank or thrift institution's files.

Credit card operations managers are responsible for the overall credit card policies and operations of a bank, commercial establishment, or credit card company. They establish procedures for verifying the information on application forms, determine applicants' creditworthiness, approve the issuance of credit cards, and set a credit limit on each account. These managers coordinate activities involved with reviewing unpaid balances, collecting delinquent accounts, investigating and preventing fraud, voiding lost or stolen credit cards, keeping records, and exchanging information with the company's branches and other credit card companies.

The *letter of credit negotiator* works with clients who hold letters of credit used in international banking. This person contacts foreign banks, suppliers, and other sources to obtain documents needed to authorize the requested loan, then checks the documents to see if they have been completed correctly so that the conditions set forth in the letter of credit meet with policy and code requirements. Before authorizing payment, the negotiator verifies the client's credit rating and may request increasing the collateral or reducing the amount of purchases, amending the contract accordingly. The letter of credit negotiator specifies the method of payment and informs the foreign bank when a loan has gone unpaid for a certain length of time.

The *trust officer* directs operations concerning the administration of private, corporate, and probate trusts. Officers examine or draft trust agreements to ensure compliance with legal requirements and terms creating trusts. They locate, inventory, and evaluate assets of probated accounts. They also direct realization of assets, liquidation of liabilities, payment of bills, preparation of federal and state tax returns on trust income, and collection of earnings. They represent the institution in trust fund negotiations.

Reserve officers maintain the institution's reserve funds according to policy and as required by law. They regulate the flow of money through branches, correspondent banks, and the Federal Reserve Bank. They also consolidate financial statements, calculate the legal reserve, and compile statistical and analytical reports of the reserves.

Foreign-exchange traders maintain the balance that the institution has on deposit in foreign banks to ensure its foreign exchange position and determine the prices at which that exchange will be purchased and sold. Their conclusions are based on an analysis of demand, supply, and the stability of the currency. They establish local rates of exchange based upon money market quotations or the customer's financial standing. They also buy and sell foreign exchange drafts and compute the proceeds.

The *securities trader* performs securities investment and counseling service for the bank and its customers. They study financial background and future trends and advise financial institution officers and customers regarding investments in stocks and bonds. They transmit buy-and-sell orders to a trading desk or broker as directed and recommend purchase, retention, or sale of issues, then notify the customer or the bank of the execution of trading orders. They compute extensions, commissions, and other charges for billing customers and making payments for securities.

The *operations officer* is in charge of the internal operations in a department or branch office of a financial institution. This person is responsible for the smooth and efficient operation of a particular area. Duties include interviewing, hiring, and directing the training of employees, as well as supervising their activities, evaluating their performance, and making certain that they comply with established procedures. Operations officers audit accounts, records, and certifications and verify the count of incoming cash. They prepare reports on the activities of the department or branch, control the supply of money for its needs, and perform other managerial tasks of a general nature.

The *credit union manager* directs the operations of credit unions, which are chartered by the state or federal government to provide savings and loan services to their members. This manager reviews loan applications, arranges automatic payroll deductions for credit union members wishing to make regular savings deposits or loan payments, and assists in collecting delinquent accounts. Managers prepare financial statements, help the government audit credit union records, and supervise bookkeeping and clerical activities. Acting as management representative of the credit union, credit union managers have the power to sign legal documents and checks on behalf of the board of directors. They also oversee control of the credit union's assets and advise the board on how to invest its funds.

Requirements

High School

You will need at least a bachelor's degree if you want to work as a financial institution officer or manager. While you are in high school, therefore, you should take classes that will give you a solid preparation for college. Such classes include mathematics, such as algebra and geometry, science, history, and a foreign language. Take English courses to improve your researching, writing, and communication skills. Also, take computer classes. Computer technology is an integral part of today's financial world, and you will benefit from being familiar with this tool. Finally, if your high school offers classes in economics, accounting, or finance, be sure to take advantage of these courses. The course work will not only give you an opportunity to gain knowlege but also allow you to see if you enjoy working with numbers and theories.

Postsecondary Training

Possible majors for you to take in college include accounting, economics, finance, or business administration with an emphasis on accounting or finance. You will need to continue honing your computer skills during this time. Also, you will probably have exposure to business law classes. It is important for you to realize that federal and state laws regarding business and finances change, so you will need to become familiar with current regulations.

Financial institutions increasingly seek candidates with master's degrees in business administration for positions as managers. So keep in mind that you may have to pursue further education even after you have completed your bachelor's degree. No matter what level of degree you obtain, however, you will also need to keep up your education even as you work. Many financial management and banking associations offer continuing education programs in conjunction with colleges or universities. These programs are geared toward advancing and updating your knowledge of subjects such as changing banking regulations, financial analysis, and international banking.

Certification or Licensing

Certification is one way to show your commitment to the field, improve your skills, and increase your possibilities for advancement. Professional certification is available in specialized fields such as investment and credit management. Investment professionals who have a bachelor's degree, have passed three test levels, and have three or more years of experience in the field can earn the Chartered Financial Analyst designation, which is conferred by the Association for Investment Management and Research. The National Association of Credit Management offers business credit professionals a three-part certification program that consists of work experience and examinations. Financial managers pass through the level of Credit Business Associate to Credit Business Fellow to Certified Credit Executive. The Association for Financial Professionals confers the Certified Cash Manager designation. Applicants must pass an examination and have working experience in the field. The Association for Financial Professionals also offers the Certified Treasury Executive designation to more advanced professionals who meet continuing education and experience requirements.

Other Requirements

In the banking business the ability to get along well with others is essential. Financial institution officers should show tact and should convey a feeling of understanding and confidence in their employees and customers. Honesty is perhaps the most important qualification for a financial institution officer. They handle large sums of money and have access to confidential financial information about the individuals and business concerns associated with their institutions. They, therefore, must have a high degree of personal integrity.

Exploring

Except for high school courses that are business-oriented, the average high school student will find few opportunities for experience and exploration during the school year. Ask your teacher or guidance counselor to arrange a class tour through a financial institution. This will at least give you a taste of how banking services work. You can gain the most valuable experience by finding a part-time or a summer job in a bank or other institution that sometimes hires qualified high school or college students. Finally, to gain some hands-on experience with managing money, consider joining a school or local club in which you could work as the treasurer.

Employers

Financial institution officers and managers work for banks and personal credit institutions such as credit unions and finance companies.

Starting Out

One way to enter banking as a regular employee is through part-time or summer employment. Anyone can apply for a position by writing to a financial institution officer in charge of personnel or by arranging for an interview appointment. Many institutions advertise in the classified section of local newspapers. The larger banks recruit on college campuses. An officer will visit a campus and conduct interviews at that time. Student placement offices can also arrange for interviews.

Advancement

There is no one method for advancement among financial institution officers. Advancement depends on the size of the institution, the services it offers, and the qualifications of the employee. Usually, the smaller the employer the slower the advancements.

Financial institutions often offer special training programs that take place at night, during the summer, and in some special instances during scheduled working hours. People who take advantage of these opportunities usually find that advancement comes more quickly. The American Banking Institute (part of the American Bankers Association), for example, offers training in every phase of banking through its own facilities or the facilities of the local universities and banking organizations. The length of this training may vary from six months to two years. Years of service and experience are required for a top-level financial institution officer to become acquainted with policy, operations, customers, and the community. Similarly, the National Association of Credit Management offers training and instruction.

Earnings

Those who enter banking in the next few years will find the earnings to be dependent on their experience, the size of the institution, and its location. In general, starting salaries in financial institutions are not usually the highest, although among larger financial institutions in big cities, starting salaries often compare favorably with salaries in large corporations. After 5 to 10 years' experience, the salaries of officers usually are slightly higher than those in large corporations for people of comparable experience.

Financial managers in commercial banks earned a median annual salary of $45,800 in 1997, according to the U.S. Department of Labor. Also according to the department, the lowest paid 10 percent of financial managers made approximately $27,680 in 1998, while the highest paid 10 percent earned around $118,950 or more in 1998. According to a 1997 survey conducted by the Association for Financial Professionals, officers and managers who have earned a master's degree or higher earn about $10,900 more than those who have only earned a bachelor's degree.

Group life insurance, paid vacations, profit sharing plans, and hospitalization and retirement plans are some of the benefits offered to financial officers and managers.

Work Environment

Working conditions in financial institutions are generally pleasant. They are usually clean, well maintained, and often air-conditioned. They are generally located throughout cities for the convenience of customers and employees, too. For financial institution officers, hours may be somewhat irregular as many organizations have expanded their hours of business.

Outlook

The number of job openings for financial institution officers and managers is expected to increase about as fast as the average for all other occupations through 2008 according to predictions by the U.S. Department of Labor. The need for skilled professionals will increase primarily as a result of greater domestic and foreign competition, changing laws affecting taxes and other financial matters, and a growing emphasis on accurate reporting of financial data for both financial institutions and corporations.

Competition for these jobs will be strong, however, for several reasons. Financial institution officers and managers are often promoted from within the ranks of the organization, and, once established in their jobs, they tend to stay for many years. Also, more qualified applicants are becoming available each year to fill the vacancies that do arise; workers who have earned a master's degree in business administration will enjoy the lowest unemployment rates. Chances for employment will be best for workers who are familiar with a range of financial services, such as banking, insurance, real estate, and securities, and for those experienced in computers and data processing systems.

For More Information

This organization has information about the banking industry and continuing education available through the American Institute of Banking. It also has information on the Stonier Graduate School of Banking.

American Bankers Association
1120 Connecticut Avenue, NW
Washington, DC 20036
Tel: 800-226-5377
Web: http://www.aba.com/

For information on the Certified Cash Manager and Certified Treasury Executive designations, contact:

Association for Financial Professionals
7315 Wisconsin Avenue, Suite 600 West
Bethesda, MD 20814
Tel: 301-907-2862
Web: http://www.afponline.org

For information on the Chartered Financial Analyst designation, contact:

Association for Investment Management and Research
PO Box 3668
560 Ray C. Hunt Drive
Charlottesville, VA 22903-0668
Tel: 800-247-8132
Email: info@aimr.org
Web: http://www.aimr.org/

For information on certification, continuing education, and general information on the banking and credit industry, contact:

National Association of Credit Management
8840 Columbia 100 Parkway
Columbia, MD 21045
Tel: 410-740-5560
Email: nacm_info@nacm.org
Web: http://www.nacm.org

Another source of continuing education in banking is the New York Institute of Finance. Contact the national headquarters at:

New York Institute of Finance
Two World Trade Center, 17th Floor
New York, NY 10048
Tel: 800-227-6943
Email: info@nyif.com
Web: http://www.nyif.com

Financial Institution Tellers

School Subjects
Business
Mathematics

Personal Skills
Communication/ideas
Following instructions

Work Environment
Primarily indoors
Primarily one location

Minimum Education Level
Some postsecondary training

Salary Range
$12,970 to $17,200 to $23,000+

Certification or Licensing
None available

Outlook
Decline

Overview

Financial institution tellers are employees of banks and other financial institutions who handle certain types of customer account transactions. At the teller window, they receive and pay out money, record customer transactions, cash checks, sell traveler's checks, and perform other banking duties. Most people are familiar with commercial tellers who cash checks and handle deposits and withdrawals from customers. Many specialized tellers are employed, too, especially in large financial institutions. Approximately 560,000 bank tellers are employed in the United States.

History

Throughout the centuries various methods of banking have been used. Although history does not record with certainty when banking first started in the world, ancient Babylonian records reflect that their people had a rather complex system of lending, borrowing, and depositing money even before 2500 BC.

In ancient times men would sit at low benches or tables in public squares to transact financial business and exchange money with customers. In fact, the word "bank" comes from the Italian word banco, meaning bench. Today, the work of tellers is in essence quite similar to that performed in ancient times: they receive money for safekeeping and pay out money on checks and drafts. The teller remains the initial contact between bank and customer, working from behind a service counter even as bankers through history worked from behind their benches in the ancient public squares.

The Job

Tellers may perform a variety of duties in their jobs, but all of these duties involve accepting and disbursing funds to customers and keeping careful records of these transactions. *Commercial tellers*, or *paying and receiving tellers*, serve the public directly by accepting customers' deposits and providing them with receipts, paying out withdrawals and recording the transactions, cashing checks, exchanging money for customers to provide them with certain kinds of change or currency, and accepting savings account deposits. When cashing checks, tellers are responsible for checking the signatures to make sure they are valid, getting a valid identification of the person cashing the check, and, in some cases, verifying that the account against which the check is drawn has enough money to cover the amount.

Tellers make sure that deposit slips, deposit receipts, and the amount entered in passbooks are correctly recorded. They must be very cautious when counting amounts of money that they pay out or accept for deposit. Machines are often used to add and subtract, make change, print records and receipts for customers' records, post transactions on ledgers, and count coins. Almost all banks today are computerized. In some large institutions with many branches, tellers use a computer linked to the main office database to conduct transactions and verify customer balances.

At the beginning of every work day, tellers are given cash drawers from the vault containing a certain amount of cash. During the day, they use this money to pay customers and add all deposited money. After their shift, tellers count the money in their cash drawers, add up the transactions they have conducted, and balance the day's accounts. If their calculations show a different amount from the money in their cash drawers, they double-check their math and account sheets. Conscientious tellers are able to balance the day's accounts to the penny every day.

Tellers may be responsible for sorting checks and deposit slips, counting and wrapping money by hand or machine, filing new-account cards, and removing closed-account cards from the files. They give customers written information about the types of services and accounts available at the bank and answer any questions. They are supervised by *head tellers* and *teller supervisors*, who train them, arrange their schedules, and monitor their records of the day's transactions, helping to reconcile any discrepancies in balancing.

In large financial institutions, tellers may be identified by the specialized types of transactions that they handle. *Note tellers* are responsible for receiving and issuing receipts or payments on promissory notes and recording these transactions correctly. *Discount tellers* are responsible for issuing and collecting customers' notes. *Foreign banknote tellers* work in the exchange department, where they buy and sell foreign currency. When customers need to trade their foreign currency for U.S. currency, these tellers determine the current value of the foreign currency in dollars, count out the bills requested by the customer, and make change. These tellers may also sell foreign currency and traveler's checks for people traveling out of the country. *Collection and exchange tellers* accept payments in forms other than cash—contracts, mortgages, and bonds, for example.

Tellers may be employed by financial institutions other than banks. These institutions include savings and loan associations, personal finance companies, credit unions, government agencies, and large businesses operating credit offices. Although the particular duties may differ among institutions, the responsibilities and need for accuracy are the same. Tellers comprise the largest specialized occupational group of bank employees.

Requirements

High School

Most banks and financial institutions require that applicants have at least a high school education. If you are interested in becoming a bank teller, take courses in high school in mathematics, business arithmetic, and even bookkeeping. These classes will give you familiarity in working with numbers. Also, it will be important for you to become comfortable using technology and working efficiently with your hands, so take computer classes, typing, and courses in business machines if these are offered in your high school. Finally, since much of this job involves working with customers, take English courses to improve your communication skills.

Postsecondary Training

Newly hired tellers at large financial institutions often receive about one week of classroom training. Following this classroom work, new tellers undergo on-the-job training, typically for several weeks, before they are allowed to work independently. Smaller financial institutions may only provide the on-the-job training in which new tellers are supervised in their work by experienced employees.

To enhance your possibility of getting a job, you may want to see if there is a community college in your area that offers preemployment training programs for those in the financial industry. Numerous educational opportunities will be available to you once you have begun working—and gaining experience—in the financial world. For example, the educational division of the American Bankers Association—the American Institute of Banking—has a vast array of adult education classes in business fields and offers training courses in numerous parts of the country that enable people to earn standard or graduate certificates in bank training. Individuals may also enroll in correspondence study courses. Other educational institutions, such as the New York Institute of Finance and the Stonier Graduate School of Banking, offer opportunities for experienced bankers to study specialized areas of banking.

Today many bank employees have a college education or have taken a number of these specialized training courses. Many individuals who have earned a college degree work as tellers to gain experience in this aspect of banking, anticipating promotions to higher positions within the bank.

Other Requirements

Desirable aptitudes for a bank teller are accuracy, speed, a good memory, the ability to work with figures, manual dexterity to handle money quickly, neatness, and orderliness. An essential prerequisite for tellers is that their honesty is above reproach, reflecting absolute trustworthiness. The work of the teller involves handling large sums of money. Therefore, bank tellers must be able to meet the standards established by bonding companies to be personally bonded as employees.

A prospective teller must be able to present a list of references that will attest to the person's good character and high standards of moral conduct. The teller must be able to work cooperatively with others and have a pleasant personality and friendly manner when working with the public. The nature of the teller's work and the bank's responsibility to its customers demand that all banking business be treated confidentially and not be discussed with anyone outside the workplace.

Exploring

You can explore this occupation in a number of ways. Summer or part-time work is frequently available, depending on the locality. Students can work in clerical jobs, as messengers, or in other positions to observe the work of tellers. You may also visit banks and other financial institutions to talk with people employed in the field.

If you are interested in working for a bank or financial institution, participating in school clubs and community activities will give you experience in working with people, handling money, and functioning as part of a team. Employers view these types of activities favorably when they consider applicants for teller positions.

Employers

Financial institution tellers are employed by banks, savings and loan associations, personal finance companies, credit unions, government agencies, and large businesses operating credit offices. There are approximately 560,000 financial institution tellers working in the United States. About one-third of this number work part time.

Starting Out

Most tellers are promoted to teller positions from beginning jobs as book-keeping or other general clerks. The skills and aptitudes people show in these beginning jobs, in addition to seniority, usually determine who will be promoted to a teller position. On the other hand, some applicants are able to obtain beginning jobs as tellers, especially in banks in large cities that offer classroom and on-the-job training programs.

Job opportunities can be found by applying in person to the institution for which you would like to work or which you have heard is hiring. Openings can also be found through newspaper help wanted ads, private or state employment agencies, or school placement services.

Advancement

Many banks and financial institutions follow a "promote-from-within" poli-cy. Promotions are usually given on the basis of past job performance and consider the employee's seniority, ability, and general personal qualities. Tellers may be promoted to head teller or other supervisory positions such as department head. Some head tellers may be transferred from the main branch bank to a smaller branch and through experience and seniority be promoted to assistant branch manager or branch manager.

Employees who show initiative in their job responsibilities, pursue additional formal education and job training, and show their ability to assume leadership may in time be promoted to junior bank officer positions. These positions include such jobs as assistant cashier, assistant trust officer, and assistant departmental vice president. Such advancements reflect a recognition of the individual's potential for even greater future job responsibilities. Advancement to the higher echelons of the bank usually require a formal college or advanced degree.

Earnings

Yearly salaries and hourly wages paid to tellers vary across the country and are usually determined by the bank's size and geographic location and the employee's experience, responsibilities, formal education, specialized training, and ability. According to the U.S. Department of Labor, full-time tellers earned a median annual income of about $17,200 in 1998. The highest-paid 10 percent made approximately $23,000 or more per year, while the lowest paid 10 percent (typically those with fewer responsibilities and in lower-paying areas of the country) made around $12,970 in 1998.

In most cases, fringe benefits for these workers are very good. Paid holidays may range from five to twelve days, depending on the bank's geographic location. Paid vacation periods vary, but many employees receive a two-week paid vacation after 1 year of service, three weeks after 10 to 15 years, and four weeks after 25 years. Group life, hospitalization, and surgical insurance plans are usually available, and employees frequently participate in shared employer-employee retirement plans. In some banks profit-sharing plans are open to employee enrollment. However, most part-time tellers are not eligible for fringe benefits such as life and health insurance.

Work Environment

Most bank employees work a 40-hour week. Tellers may sometimes be required to work irregular hours or overtime. Many banks stay open until 8:00 PM on Friday nights to accommodate the large number of workers who receive paychecks on that day. Part-time work for tellers is increasingly available.

Banks and financial institutions are usually pleasant places in which to work. Office equipment and furnishings are usually modern, and efforts are made to create a relaxed but efficient work atmosphere. Although tellers usually do not perform any physically strenuous work, they may have to stand at their stations for long periods of time. Dealing with customers may be tiring, especially during busy periods or when customers are difficult or demanding.

Outlook

The U.S. Department of Labor predicts a decline in employment of financial institution tellers through 2008. There are a couple of reasons for this projected decline. In recent years, overexpansion by banks and competition from companies that offer bank-like services have resulted in closings, mergers, and consolidations in the banking industry. Furthermore, the rate of employment for tellers is not expected to keep pace with overall employment growth in other banking occupations because of the increasing use of automatic teller machines, banking by telephone and computer, and other technologies that increase teller efficiency or remove the need for tellers altogether.

Most employment opportunities will arise from the need to replace those workers who have left the field. This occupation provides a relatively large number of job openings due to its large size and high turnover rate. Demand for part-time tellers, especially during peak periods, is expected to be particularly strong. The field of banking offers a greater degree of job stability than some other fields as it is less likely to be affected by dips in the general economy.

For More Information

This organization has information about the banking industry and continuing education available through the American Institute of Banking. It also has information on the Stonier Graduate School of Banking.

American Bankers Association
1120 Connecticut Avenue, NW
Washington, DC 20036
Tel: 800-226-5377
Web: http://www.aba.com/

The Bank Administration Institute (BAI) has information on continuing education and seminars in banking.

Bank Administration Institute
One North Franklin, Suite 1000
Chicago, IL 60606-3421
Tel: 800-224-9889
Email: info@bai.org
Web: http://www.bai.org

The Institute, which joined forces with BAI in 1999, offers a wide variety of publications and continuing education and training opportunities for financial institution workers.

The Institute of Financial Education
55 West Monroe, Suite 2800
Chicago, IL 60603-5014
Tel: 800-946-0488
Web: http://www.bai.org/ife

The New York Institute of Finance offers many education programs for those in the finance industry. Contact the national headquarters at:

New York Institute of Finance
Two World Trade Center, 17th Floor
New York, NY 10048
Tel: 800-227-6943
Email: info@nyif.com
Web: http://www.nyif.com

Financial Planners

Business Mathematics	School Subjects
Helping/teaching Leadership/management	Personal Skills
Primarily indoors Primarily one location	Work Environment
Bachelor's degree	Minimum Education Level
$18,000 to $110,000 to $200,000+	Salary Range
Recommended	Certification or Licensing
Faster than the average	Outlook

Overview

Financial planning is the process of establishing financial goals and creating ways to reach them. *Financial planners* examine the assets of their clients and suggest what steps they need to take in the future to meet their goals. They take a broad approach to financial advice, which distinguishes them from other professional advisors, such as insurance agents, stockbrokers, accountants, attorneys, and real estate agents, each of whom typically focuses on only one aspect of a person's finances.

History

Bombarded with investment ads, more investors are turning to professionals to recommend strategies for their financial futures. The amount of assets managed by fee-only financial planners, which are nearly one quarter of all financial planners and the fastest-growing segment of the industry, has doubled to $282 billion during the period of 1994-99, according to *U.S. News*

Online. The profession is booming because of increased competition by banks, brokerages, and mutual funds, all of which want to expand their financial planning services for individuals and small businesses.

The increased amount of information on financial planning due to the Internet has had an interesting affect on certified financial planners. In a 1998 survey, 55 percent of the respondents thought that the Internet increased the information and available data they used in making recommendations to their customers, yet fewer (49 percent) thought that the Internet actually increased the quality of information available. Only one in four survey respondents indicated that the performance of their clients' investments had improved as a result of information available through the Internet practitioners, according to the College of Financial Planning. About half of present certified financial planners use the Internet, while about one-third do not think they have benefited from it, and a remaining 14 percent do not use it at all.

The Job

Financial planners advise their clients on many aspects of finance. Although they seem to be jacks of all trades, certified financial planners do not work alone; they meet with their clients' other advisors, such as attorneys, accountants, trust officers, and investment bankers. Gathering this research helps financial planners to fully understand their clients' overall financial picture. After meeting with the clients and their other advisors, certified financial planners analyze the data they have received and generate a written report that includes their recommendations on how the clients can best achieve their goals. This report details the clients' financial objectives, current income, investments, risk tolerance, expenses, tax returns, insurance coverage, retirement programs, estate plans, and other important information.

Financial planning is an ongoing process. The plan must be monitored and reviewed periodically so that adjustments can be made, if necessary, to assure that it continues to meet individual needs.

The plan itself is a set of recommendations and strategies for clients to use or ignore, according to *The Princeton Review Online*, and financial planners should be ready to answer hard questions about the integrity of the plans they map out. After all, they are dealing with all of the money and investments that people have worked a lifetime accruing.

People need financial planners for different things. Some might want life insurance, college savings plans, or estate planning. Sometimes these needs are triggered by changes in people's lives, such as retirement, death of a spouse, disability, marriage, birth of children, or job changes. Certified financial planners spend the majority of their time on the following topics: investment planning, retirement planning, tax planning, estate planning, and risk management. All of these areas require different types of financial knowledge, and planners are generally expected to be extremely competent in the disciplines of asset management, employee benefits, estate planning, insurance, investments, and retirement, according to the Institute of Certified Financial Planners. A financial planner must also have good interpersonal skills, since establishing solid client-planner relationships is essential to the planners' success. It also helps to have good communications skills, since even the best financial plan, if presented poorly to a client, can be rejected.

The job of financial planner is driven by clients. The advice they provide depends on their clients' particular needs, resources, and priorities. Many people think they cannot afford or do not need a comprehensive financial plan. Certified financial planners must have a certain amount of expertise in sales to build their client base.

Certified financial planners use various ways to develop their client lists, including telephone solicitation, giving seminars on financial planning to the general public or specific organizations, and networking with social contacts. Referrals from satisfied customers also help the business' growth.

Although certified financial planners are trained in comprehensive financial planning, some specialize in one area, such as asset management, investments, or retirement planning. In most small or self-owned financial planning companies, they are generalists. However, in some large companies, planners might specialize in particular areas, including insurance, real estate, mutual funds, annuities, pensions, or business valuations.

Requirements

High School

If financial planning sounds interesting to you, take as many business classes as possible, as well as mathematics. Communications courses, such as speech or drama, will help put you at ease when talking in front of a crowd—something financial planners must do occasionally. English courses will help you prepare the written reports planners present to their clients.

Postsecondary Training

Earning a bachelor's degree starts financial planners on the right track, but it will help if your degree indicates a skill with numbers, be it in science or business. A business administration degree with a specialization in financial planning or a liberal arts degree with courses in accounting, business administration, economics, finance, marketing, human behavior, counseling, and public speaking is excellent preparation for this sort of job.

Certification or Licensing

However, education alone will not motivate clients to easily turn over their finances to you. Many financial professionals are licensed on the state and federal levels within subsets of financial planning, such as stocks and insurance, but with few exceptions, they are not regulated for their financial planning activities. Therefore, most financial planners have chosen to become certified by the Certified Financial Board of the Institute of Certified Financial Planners.

Most Certified Financial Planner (CFP) professionals have earned four-year degrees in areas such as accounting, economics, business administration, marketing, or finance. They have also completed a course of study in financial planning at one of the more than 80 colleges or universities that have registered its education program with the CFP Board. Successful completion of one of these programs automatically satisfies the education component of the CFP certification process.

To become licensed to use the CFP mark, individuals must meet what the CFP Board refers to as the four E's, which comprise the following. Examination—individuals must successfully complete the CFP Board's comprehensive certification examination, which tests knowledge on various key aspects of financial planning. Experience—depending on the level of degree work completed in a collegiate setting, prospects must acquire three to five years of financial planning-related experience prior to receiving the right to use the CFP mark. Ethics—they must voluntarily ascribe to the CFP Board's Code of Ethics and additional requirements as mandated from time to time. This decision empowers the board to take action if a CFP licensee violates the Code of Ethics. Such valuations could lead to disciplinary action, including permanent revocation of the right to use the CFP mark. Education—a CFP licensee must obtain 30 hours of continuing education every two years in areas such as estate planning, retirement planning, investment management, tax planning, employee benefits, and insurance.

The Securities and Exchange Commission and most states have licensing requirements for investment advisors, a category under which most financial planners also fall.

Other Requirements

Other things that are attributed to success as a financial planner include keeping up with continuing education, referrals from clients, specialization, people and communication skills, and a strong educational background.

Exploring

There is not much that students can do to explore this field, since success as a certified financial planner comes only with training and years on the job. However, you can check out the financial planning information available on the Internet to familiarize yourself with the terms used in the industry. You should also take as many finance and business classes as possible. Talking to certified financial planners will also help you gather information on the field.

Employers

Financial planners are employed by financial planning firms across the country. Many of these firms are small, perhaps employing 2 to 15 people, and most are located in urban areas. A smaller, but growing, number of financial planners is employed by corporations, banks, credit unions, mutual fund companies, insurance companies, accounting or law firms, colleges and universities, credit counseling organizations, and brokerage firms. In addition, many financial planners are self-employed.

Starting Out

Early in their careers, financial planners work for banks, mutual fund companies, or investment firms and will receive extensive on-the-job training. The job will deal heavily with client-based and research activities. Financial planners may start their own business as they learn personal skills and build their client base. During the first two years, certified financial planners spend many hours analyzing documents, meeting with other advisors, and networking to find new clients.

Advancement

Those who have not changed their career track in five years can expect to have established some solid, long-term relationships with clients. Measured success at this point will be the planner's service fees, which will be marked up considerably from when they started.

Those who have worked in the industry for 10 years usually have many clients, a good track record, and a six-figure income. Experienced financial planners can also move into careers in investment banking, financial consulting, and financial analysis. Because people skills are also an integral part of being a financial planner, consulting—on both personal and corporate levels—are also options. Many planners will find themselves attending business school, either to achieve a higher income or to switch to one of the aforementioned professions.

Earnings

There are several methods of compensation for financial planners. "Fee-only" means that compensation is entirely from fees from consultation, plan development, or investment management. These fees may be charged on an hourly or project basis depending on clients' needs, or on a percentage of assets under management. "Commission only" compensation is received from the sale of financial products that clients agree to purchase to implement financial planning recommendations. There is no charge for advice or preparation of the financial plan. "Fee-offset" means that compensation received in the form of commission from the sale of financial products is offset against fees charged for the planning process. "Combination fee/commission" is a fee charged for consultation, advice, and financial plan preparation on an hourly, project, or percentage basis. Planners might also receive commissions from recommended products targeted to achieve goals and objectives. Some planners work on a "salary" basis for financial services institutions such as banks, credit unions, and other related organizations.

The salary range for certified financial planners is $50,000 to $111,000 to $200,000 or more, according to the annual *Survey of Trends in Financial Planning* conducted by the College of Financial Planning. These incomes were earned from financial plan writing, product sales, consulting, and related activities.

Another survey, conducted by the National Endowment for Financial Education, reports that entry level planners earn $18,000, while experienced, certified planners earn over $100,000 annually.

Firms might also provide beginning financial planners with a steady income by paying a draw, which is a minimum salary based on the commission and fees for which the planner can be expected to earn.

Some financial planners receive vacation days, sick days, and health insurance, but that depends on if they work for financial institutions, or on their own.

The median hourly rate for financial planners who charge by the hour is $116 in 1999, according to the Certified Financial Planner Board of Standards.

Work Environment

Most financial planners work by themselves in offices or at home. Others work in offices with other financial planners. Established financial planners usually work the same hours as the business community. Beginners who are seeking customers probably work longer hours. Many planners accommodate customers by meeting with them in the evenings and on weekends. They might spend a lot of time out of the office meeting with current and prospective clients, attending civic functions, and participating in trade association meetings.

Outlook

The employment of financial planners is expected to grow rapidly in the future for a number of reasons. More funds should be available for investment, as the economy, personal income, and inherited wealth grow. Demographics will also play a role; as increasing numbers of baby boomers (people born between 1946 and 1964) turn 50, demand will grow for retirement-related investments. Most people, in general, are likely to turn to financial planners for assistance with retirement planning. Individual saving and investing for retirement are expected to become more important, as many companies reduce pension benefits and switch from defined-benefit retirement plans to defined-contribution plans, which shift the investment responsibility from the company to the individual. Furthermore, a growing number of individual investors are expected to seek advice from financial planners regarding the increasing complexity and array of investment alternatives for assistance with estate planning.

Due to the highly competitive nature of financial planning, many beginners leave the field because they are not able to establish a sufficient clientele. Once established, however, planners have a strong attachment to their occupation because of high earning potential and considerable investment in training. Job opportunities should be best for mature individuals with successful work experience.

For More Information

To obtain information on certification and a copy of their General Information Book, *contact:*

Certified Financial Planner Board of Standards
1700 Broadway, Suite 2100
Denver, CO 80290-2101
Tel: 303-830-7500
Email: mail@CFP-Board.org
Web: http://www.cfp-board.org

For information on educational opportunities, contact:

College of Financial Planning
6161 South Syracuse Way
Greenwood Village, CO 80111-4707
Tel: 303-220-1200
Web: http://www.fp.edu

For information on the Certified Financial Planner designation, contact:

Financial Planning Association
Tel: 800-322-4237
Web: http://www.fpanet.org

Financial Services Brokers

School Subjects	Business Mathematics
Personal Skills	Communication/ideas Technical/scientific
Work Environment	Primarily indoors Primarily one location
Minimum Education Level	Bachelor's degree
Salary Range	$18,100 to $38,800 to $98,400+
Certification or Licensing	Required by certain states
Outlook	Much faster than the average

Overview

Financial services brokers, sometimes called *registered representatives, account executives, securities sales representatives,* or *stockbrokers,* work to represent both individuals and organizations who wish to invest in and sell stocks, bonds, or other financial products. Financial services brokers analyze companies offering stocks to see if investing in them is worth the risk. They also advise clients on proper investment strategies for their own investment goals.

History

When a government wants to build a new sewer system or a company wants to build a new factory, it rarely has the required money—or capital—readily at hand to do it. It must first raise the capital from investors. Historically, raising capital to finance the needs of government and commerce was—and often still is—an arduous task. European monarchies, particularly during the 18th and 19th centuries, relied heavily upon bankers to meet the costs of the interminable wars that devastated the Continent and to assist in early industrial expansion. This system grew obsolete, however, and governments, banks, and industry turned to the burgeoning middle class for funds. They offered middle class investors securities and stocks—a fractional ownership in a company or enterprise—in exchange for their money. Soon, dealers emerged that linked government and industry with the smaller investor. In the United States, the New York Stock Exchange was formed in 1790 and officially established in 1817.

The stock exchange functions as a marketplace where stockbrokers buy and sell securities for individuals or institutions. Stock prices can fluctuate from minute to minute, with the price of a stock at any given time determined by the demand for it. As a direct result of the disastrous stock market crash of 1929, the Federal Securities Act of 1934 set up a federal commission to control the handling of securities and made illegal any manipulation of prices on stock exchanges. Today the public is protected by regulations that set standards for stock listings, require public disclosure of the financial condition of companies offering stock, and prohibit stock manipulation and trading on inside information.

The Job

The most important part of a broker's job is finding customers and building a client base. Beginning brokers spend much of their time searching for customers, relying heavily on telephone solicitation "cold calls"—that is, calling people with whom they have never had any contact. They may also find customers through business and social contacts or be given a list of likely prospects from their brokerage firm.

When they open accounts for new customers, they first record all the personal information that is required to allow the customer to trade securities through the brokerage firm. Depending on a customer's knowledge of the market, the broker may explain the meaning of stock market terms and trading practices; offer financial counseling; and devise an individual financial portfolio for the customer, including securities, life insurance, corporate and municipal bonds, mutual funds, certificates of deposit, annuities, and other investments. The broker must determine the customer's investment goals—whether the customer wants long-term, steady growth or a quick turnaround of stocks for short-term gains—and then offers advice on investments accordingly. Once an investment strategy has been worked out, brokers execute buy and sell orders for their customers by relaying the information to the floor of the stock exchange, where the order is actually put into effect by a broker's floor representative. *Securities traders* also buy and sell securities, but usually as a representative of a private firm.

From the research department of the brokerage firm, brokers obtain information on the activities and projected growth of any company that is offering or will offer stock. The actual or perceived strength of a company is a major factor in a stock-purchase decision. Brokers must be prepared to answer questions on the technical aspects of stock market operations and also be informed on current economic conditions. They are expected to have the market knowledge to anticipate certain trends and to counsel customers accordingly in terms of their particular stock holdings.

Some financial services brokers specialize in specific areas such as handling only institutional accounts, bond issues, or mutual funds. Whatever their area of specialization, financial services brokers must keep abreast of all significant political and economic conditions, maintain very accurate records for all transactions, and continually solicit new customers.

Requirements

High School

If you are interested in becoming a financial services broker, you should take courses in business, accounting, economics, mathematics, government, and communications.

Postsecondary Training

Because of the specialized knowledge necessary to perform this job properly, a college education is increasingly important, especially in the larger brokerage houses. To make intelligent and insightful judgments, a broker must be able to read and understand financial reports and evaluate statistics. For this reason, although employers seldom require specialized academic training, a bachelor's degree in business administration, economics, or finance is helpful.

Certification or Licensing

Almost all states require brokers to be licensed. Some states administer written examinations and some require brokers to post a personal bond. Beginning brokers must register as representatives of their firms in accordance with the regulations set forth by the securities exchange where they do business or the National Association of Securities Dealers (NASD). In order to qualify as registered representatives, brokers must first pass the General Securities Registered Representative Examination, administered by the NASD. Many states require brokers to take and pass a second examination—the Uniform Securities Agents State Law Examination.

Other Requirements

Because they deal with the public, brokers should be well groomed and pleasant and have large reserves of tact and patience. Employers look for ambitious individuals with sales ability. Brokers also need self-confidence and the ability to handle frequent rejections. Above all, they must have a highly developed sense of responsibility, because in many instances they will be handling funds that represent a client's life savings.

Exploring

Any sales experience can provide you with a general background for work in financial services. Occasionally, young people can find summer employment in a brokerage house. A visit to a local investment office, the New York Stock Exchange, or one of the commodities exchanges located in other major cities will provide a valuable opportunity to observe how transactions are handled and what is required of people in the field.

Employers

Financial services brokers work in brokerage and investment firms all around the country. Although many of these firms are very small, the largest employers of financial services brokers are a few large firms that have their main offices in major cities, especially New York.

Starting Out

Many firms hire beginning workers in sales, train them, and then retain them for a probationary period to determine their talents and ability to succeed. The training period lasts about six months and includes classroom instruction and on-the-job training. Applications for these beginning jobs may be made directly to the personnel offices of the various securities firms. Check your local Yellow Pages or the Internet for listings of securities firms.

Advancement

Depending upon their skills and ambitions, financial services brokers may advance rapidly in this field. Accomplished brokers may find that the size and number of accounts they service will increase to a point at which they no longer need to solicit new customers. Others become branch managers, research analysts, or partners in their own firms.

Earnings

The salaries of trainees and beginners range from $1,200 to $1,500 per month, although larger firms pay a somewhat higher starting wage. Eventually, the broker works solely on commission, with fees depending on the size and type of security bought or sold. Some firms pay annual bonuses to their brokers when business warrants. Since earnings can fluctuate greatly based on the condition of the market, some brokers may find it necessary to supplement their income through other means during times of slow market activity.

According to the U.S. Department of Labor, the median earnings for brokers were $48,090 a year in 1998; the middle 50 percent earned between $31,400 and $103,040. Ten percent earned less than $22,660 and 10 percent earned more than $124,800.

Work Environment

Brokers work more flexible hours than workers in other fields. They may work fewer hours during dull trading periods but be required to put in overtime dealing with paperwork during busy periods.

The atmosphere of a brokerage firm is frequently highly charged, and the peaks and drops of market activity can produce a great deal of tension.

Outlook

The U.S. Department of Labor predicts that job opportunities for financial services brokers are expected to grow much faster than the average for all occupations through 2008 because of continued interest in the stock market. The strong growth of the economy, rising personal incomes, and greater inherited wealth are increasing the amount of funds people are able to invest. Many people dabble in investing via their personal computers and the Internet. Even those with limited means have the option of investing through a variety of methods such as investment clubs, mutual funds, and monthly payment plans. In addition, the expansion of business activities and new technological breakthroughs will create increased demand for the sale of stock to meet capital requirements for companies around the world.

Demand for financial services brokers fluctuates with the economy. Turnover among beginners is high because they have a hard time soliciting enough clients. Because of potentially high earnings, competition in this business is very intense.

For More Information

For information on the General Securities Registered Representative Examination and other career information, contact:

National Association of Securities Dealers
9513 Key West Avenue
Rockville, MD 20850-3389
Tel: 301-590-6500
Web: http://www.nasd.com

For information on the securities industry, contact:

The Securities Industry Association
120 Broadway, 35th Floor
New York, NY 10271-0080
Tel: 212-608-1500
Web: http://www.sia.com

Forensic Accountants and Auditors

Business Mathematics	School Subjects
Communication/ideas Leadership/management	Personal Skills
Primarily indoors One location with some travel	Work Environment
Bachelor's degree	Minimum Education Level
$20,600 to $41,250 to $91,000+	Salary Range
Recommended	Certification or Licensing
About as fast as the average	Outlook

Overview

Forensic accountants and auditors, sometimes known as investigative accountants, investigative auditors, and certified fraud examiners, use accounting principles and theories to support or oppose claims being made in litigation. Like other accountants and auditors, forensic accountants are trained to analyze and verify financial records. Forensic accountants, however, use these skills to identify and document financial wrongdoing. They prepare reports that may be used in criminal and civil trials. The word "forensic" means "suitable for a court of law, public debate, or formal argumentation." There are approximately 1,080,000 accountants and auditors, which includes forensic accountants and auditors, employed in the United States.

History

People have used accounting and bookkeeping procedures for as long as they have engaged in trade. Records of accounts have been preserved from ancient and medieval times.

Modern bookkeeping dates back to the advent of double-entry bookkeeping, a method of tracking the impact of transactions on both a company's assets and profitability. Double-entry bookkeeping was developed in medieval Italy. The earliest-known published work about this system was written in 1494 by an Italian monk named Luca Pacioli (c. 1450-c. 1520). Pacioli did not invent the system, but he did summarize principles that remain largely unchanged today.

Records preserved from 16th century Europe indicate that formulations were developed during that time to account for assets, liabilities, and income. When the Industrial Revolution swept through the world in the 18th century, accounting became even more sophisticated to accommodate the acceleration of financial transactions caused by mechanization and mass production.

In the 20th century, accounting has become a more creative and interesting discipline. Computers now perform many routine computations, while accountants tend to interpret the results. Many accountants now hold senior management positions within large organizations. They assess the possible impact of various transactions, mergers, and acquisitions and help companies manage their employees more efficiently.

While people have probably investigated financial records for as long as people have kept accounts, forensic accounting did not emerge as a distinct area of specialty until quite recently. "Forensic accounting is basically a phenomenon of the past 10 years," notes Tom Fox, a forensic accountant with Davidson, Fox & Co., "though I'm sure people were using some of the same skills before that time." The increased litigation and white-collar crime of the 1980s contributed to the rapid growth of this field.

The Job

Forensic accountants and auditors have all the skills possessed by traditional accountants and auditors. They are trained to compile, verify, and analyze financial records and taxes. They can monitor the efficiency of business procedures and management. Unlike traditional accountants, however, forensic accountants use their skills to help clients prepare for trials.

"Forensic accounting," says Jim DiGabriele, of DiGabriele, McNulty & Co., "uses investigative skills to follow paper trails. We follow financial documents to the end of the trail and then we more or less prepare reports for litigation."

In an investigation, the forensic accountant usually begins by reviewing relevant financial and business documents and interviewing the people involved. He or she also may assemble relevant third-party information, such as economic data for comparable industries or companies. Using the compiled information, the forensic accountant may then calculate the losses or damages caused by any financial violations or errors. Finally, the forensic accountant prepares a detailed report explaining his or her findings and conclusions. This report is intended for use in litigation.

"Only about one in 20 cases actually goes to litigation," notes Fox, "but a forensic accountant must treat each and every report as if it is going to trial. Forensic accountants must carefully document and date every related conversation and scrap of information."

If a case is scheduled to proceed to litigation, the attorneys involved may schedule a deposition. A deposition is a pretrial hearing, in which attorneys from both sides may interview one another's witnesses to gain information about the case. Forensic accountants sometimes help attorneys prepare questions for these depositions. They also are sometimes asked to answer questions in a deposition.

If and when a case finally goes to trial, a forensic accountant also may serve as an expert witness. An expert witness is an independent authority who testifies in a trial. Forensic accountants may offer testimony regarding the nature of the violation, a person's or company's guilt or innocence, and the amount of the resulting damages. As expert witnesses, forensic accountants must be able to present information in a clear and organized manner. They must be able to explain complicated accounting concepts in a way that can be understood by people who are not in the field. They must be able to explain and defend the methods they used to arrive at their conclusions.

There is no "typical" case for a forensic accountant. Forensic accountants use their skills to investigate a wide variety of situations or violations.

Many insurance companies hire forensic accountants to evaluate claims they suspect may be inflated or fraudulent. If an insured company files a claim for a business interruption loss, for example, the insurance company may hire a forensic accountant to make sure the company's loss was as great as the company claims it was. To make this assessment, the forensic accountant must review the company's past financial records. Before calculating the company's probable loss, the forensic accountant also must consider the current marketplace. If the economy is booming and the market for the company's products or services is hot, the insured's losses may be substantial. If the economy is sluggish, or if the company's product has become obsolete, the losses may be quite a bit lower.

Insurance companies also hire forensic accountants to assess claimants' loss of income due to accidents or disability, or property loss to fire, flood, or theft. Occasionally, a claimant may hire a forensic accountant to defend his or her claim or to rebut another forensic accountant's testimony.

Forensic accountants also investigate malpractice claims against accountants or auditors. They do so by examining the reports prepared by these professionals to determine whether the accountant or auditor followed accepted procedures. If the forensic accountant does discover an error, he or she also may be required to calculate the financial impact of the discrepancy.

Companies sometimes hire forensic accountants to determine whether employees are taking kickbacks from vendors or customers in return for offering higher payments or lower prices. Companies also hire forensic accountants to detect insider trading. Insider trading occurs when an employee uses privileged information to make a profit—or helps someone else make a profit—by buying or selling stock. Forensic accountants also assist corporate clients by calculating loss due to breach of contract, patent infringement, and fraud.

Some forensic accountants engage in divorce valuation work. These professionals determine the value of the personal assets, liabilities, pensions, and business holdings of individuals involved in a divorce settlement.

Requirements

High School

If you are interested in entering this fascinating field, take as many math and computer classes as possible in high school. You also should take any available business classes, because forensic accountants must understand basic business procedures in order to assess business interruption losses. Forensic accountants who eventually form their own accounting firms also will need management and administrative skills. Business classes can offer you a solid foundation in these areas.

Writing, speech, and communications classes are extremely useful—and all too frequently neglected—courses for future forensic accountants. A forensic accountant's value to clients depends entirely on his or her ability to provide credible reports and convincing testimony for trial. For this reason, forensic accountants must be able to write clear, organized reports. They must be able to speak clearly and audibly in courtrooms. They must appear poised and confident when speaking publicly, and they must be able to convey complicated information in comprehensible language.

Postsecondary Training

Once in college, prospective forensic accountants should study accounting or business administration with a minor in accounting. "Mind you," says Fox, "you don't get out of college as a forensic accountant. You get out of college ready to be an accountant and then you learn forensic techniques through experience." Also included in your course of study should be computer classes, so that you can continue to hone your skills with this tool, as well as English or communication classes.

Some organizations prefer to hire accountants with master's degrees in accounting or master's in business administration. So, depending on what company you want to work for, you may need to continue your education beyond the college level.

Certification or Licensing

Anyone who is interested in becoming a forensic accountant should first become a Certified Public Accountant (CPA). While it is theoretically possible to practice as a forensic accountant without becoming a CPA, it is extremely unlikely that anyone would succeed in so doing. Clients hire forensic accountants with the idea that they may eventually serve as expert witnesses. A forensic accountant who was not a CPA could be easily discredited in a trial.

Most states require CPAs to have completed 150 credit hours, or the equivalent of a master's degree. The American Institute of Certified Public Accountants is working to make this a national standard for accounting education as accounting procedures and reporting laws become increasingly more complex. CPAs also must pass a grueling qualifying examination and hold a certificate issued by the state in which they wish to practice. Most states require prospective CPAs to have at least two years of experience as a public accountant before taking the qualifying examination. Most states also require CPAs to earn about 40 hours of continuing education each year.

A CPA who has gained some experience may want to consider becoming a Certified Fraud Examiner (CFE). Forensic accountants and fraud examiners use many of the same skills. In fact, the titles are sometimes used interchangeably, although, according to the National Association of Forensic Accountants, fraud examiners are more often concerned with developing procedures and implementing measures to prevent fraud. The two areas are not mutually exclusive, however; many forensic accountants also work as fraud examiners and vice versa. A CPA may gain the CFE designation by successfully completing the Uniform CFE Examination, which is administered by the National Association of Certified Fraud Examiners. The designation can help forensic accountants establish their credibility as expert witnesses. CFEs must complete at least 20 hours of continuing education each year.

The National Association of Forensic Accountants also offers training programs designed to equip CPAs to conduct forensic investigations.

Other Requirements

Forensic accountants are the sleuths of the financial world. Consequently, they must be curious and dogged in their pursuit of answers. They must have exceptional attention to detail and be capable of intense concentration. Like every professional involved with the judicial system, they frequently are subject to abrupt schedule changes so they also should be able to work under stressful conditions and meet exceptionally tight deadlines. They also must have excellent communication skills and they must be poised and confident.

Exploring

Opportunities for high school students to explore this field are limited. You may, however, contact people in this field to request information interviews. Information interviews can be an excellent way to learn about different careers. Try landing a summer job performing clerical tasks for accounting or law firms. This experience can help you become familiar with the documentation necessary in both fields.

College students should seek internship positions within accounting firms in order to gain practical experience, and to make contacts within the industry.

Employers

Forensic accountants and auditors usually work for accounting companies that provide litigation support for insurance companies, law firms, and other parties involved in litigation.

Starting Out

Most people spend several years working as accountants before specializing in forensic accounting. Their first hurdle after college is to find employment as an accountant. College professors and career placement counselors can help accounting majors arrange interviews with respected accounting firms and government agencies. Students also can contact these firms and agencies directly to learn about job opportunities. Many accounting firms and government positions are advertised in newspapers and on the Internet.

In general, accounting firms tend to offer better starting salaries than government agencies. Larger firms also sometimes have entire departments dedicated to litigation support services. New graduates who secure positions with these firms might have opportunities to learn the forensic ropes while gaining experience as accountants. With time, after earning a CPA and gaining experience, an accountant within a large firm may have an opportunity to specialize in litigation support and forensic accounting. The five largest accounting firms, collectively known as the "Big Five," are Arthur Andersen, Ernst & Young, Deloitte & Touche, KPMG, and PricewaterhouseCoopers.

Another excellent way to gain relevant experience is by working for the Internal Revenue Service (IRS). IRS auditors and accountants use many of the same skills necessary for forensic accountants. Jim DiGabriele and his partner both worked as IRS auditors before leaving to form their own forensic accounting firm.

Advancement

Forensic accountants usually advance by gaining experience and establishing reputations for integrity, thorough documentation, and reliable calculations. As a forensic accountant gains experience, he or she usually attracts more clients and is able to work on more interesting, complex cases. Experienced forensic accountants also can charge more per hour for their services, though, unless the forensic accountant is self-employed, this increase does not usually benefit the professional directly. With experience, a forensic accountant also may gain opportunities to manage a litigation support department or to become a partner in an accounting firm. A significant number of forensic accountants also advance by leaving larger firms to establish their own companies.

Earnings

While there are no salary statistics specifically for forensic accountants, most forensic accountants work within accounting firms and earn salaries that are commensurate with those of other accountants.

According to a survey conducted by the National Association of Colleges and Employers, entry-level accountants who had bachelor's degrees received average starting salaries of $34,500 in 1999. Those with master's degrees had starting salaries of $36,800 in 1999.

Robert Half International, a staffing services firm specializing in accounting and finance, reported that in 1999 individuals with up to one year of accounting experience earned between $26,000 and $36,250. Those with one to three years of experience earned between $29,250 and $41,250. Senior accountants and auditors made between $34,750 and $51,000 while managers earned between $41,750 and $68,500. Directors in this field made between $56,250 and $91,000 in 1999. Partners in accounting firms can make even more. Naturally, salaries are affected by such factors as size of the firm, the level of the accountant's education, and any certification the accountant may have.

Government positions typically offer somewhat lower salaries than other positions. According to the U.S. Department of Labor, the average starting annual salary for junior accountants and auditors in the federal government was $20,600 in 1999. Candidates who had master's degrees or two years of experience could earn $31,200 to start. More experienced accountants in the federal government made about $58,200 per year in 1999.

As forensic accountants become more experienced, they may earn slightly more than accountants earn because many firms tend to charge premium rates for litigation support services. A forensic accountant's salary and bonus figures usually reflect, at least to some degree, the revenue they are generating for the accounting firm. For this reason, a forensic accountant's salary tends to grow as he or she gains experience. According to the National Association of Forensic Accountants, forensic accountants who had fewer than 10 years of experience charged between $80 and $140 per hour for their services. About 25 percent of those who had 11 to 15 years of experience charged between $141 and $170 per hour and another 25 percent charged more than $170. Practitioners with between 16 and 20 years of experience charged between $171 and $200. In addition, 30 percent of those with more than 20 years of experience charged more than $200.

Most forensic accountants are employees who receive standard benefits such as paid vacation and sick days, health insurance, and 401(k) savings plans. Many who work for major accounting firms can also expect to earn bonuses based on their performance and the overall performance of the firm. Forensic accountants who become partners also may earn shares in the firm. Forensic accountants who act as self-employed consultants typically will not receive benefits and will have to provide their own health insurance and retirement plan.

Work Environment

Forensic accountants typically work in bright, clean offices. A great deal of their work is done on computers and telephones, though most also must occasionally travel to the offices of clients or those under investigation.

Because forensic accountants are hired to help clients prepare for trial, they often must work under tremendous pressure. They frequently encounter tight deadlines and changing schedules. Though forensic accountants generally work normal 40-hour weeks, they often must work much longer hours as they prepare for a trial.

Forensic accountants also must contend with the pressures of serving as expert witnesses. Whenever they take the stand, they know that the attorneys for the other side of a case will attempt to discredit them and question their procedures and conclusions. Forensic accountants must be prepared to undergo extremely aggressive questioning. They must be able to remain calm and confident under trying circumstances.

Outlook

The U.S. Department of Labor predicts the field of accounting to grow about as fast as the average for all occupations through 2008. As the economy grows, more accountants will be needed to prepare books and taxes for new and growing companies. New accountants also will be needed to replace those who retire or change professions. Since over one million people currently work as accountants, the number of positions created by normal turnover should be significant.

Unfortunately, there is no information that pertains specifically to forensic accounting. Most people in this field tend to believe that it will continue to grow, however. In *Careers in Accounting*, Lawrence Rosenthal identifies forensic accounting as an area experiencing increased demands.

For More Information

Because forensic accountants are almost always Certified Public Accountants, the American Institute of Certified Public Accountants and other organizations for accountants can be excellent sources of additional information.

American Institute of Certified Public Accountants
1211 Avenue of the Americas
New York, NY 10036-8775
Tel: 212-596-6200
Web: http://www.aicpa.org

For information on scholarships, continuing education, student membership, and the CFE designation, contact:

National Association of Certified Fraud Examiners
The Gregor Building
716 West Avenue
Austin, TX 78701
Tel: 800-245-3321
Email: info@cfenet.com
Web: http://www.cfenet.com

For information on investigative accounting, contact:

National Association of Forensic Accountants
2455 East Sunrise Boulevard, Suite 1201
Fort Lauderdale, FL 33304
Tel: 800-523-3680
Email: info@nafanet.com
Web: http://www.claimsupport.com/nafanet.com

For information on membership, scholarships, and continuing education, contact:

National Society of Accountants
1010 North Fairfax Street
Alexandria, VA 22314
Tel: 703-549-6400
Web: http://www.nsacct.org

Insurance Claims Representatives

Business Mathematics	School Subjects
Following instructions Leadership/management	Personal Skills
Indoors and outdoors One location with some travel	Work Environment
Bachelor's degree	Minimum Education Level
$24,010 to $38,290 to $55,000	Salary Range
Required by certain states	Certification or Licensing
About as fast as the average	Outlook

Overview

Insurance claims representatives, or *claims adjusters*, investigate claims for personal, casualty, or property loss or damages. They determine the extent of the insurance company's liability and try to negotiate an out-of-court settlement with the claimant.

History

Insurance is an action or process that insures a party against loss or damage by a contingent event, such as fire, accident, illness, or death. The field originated in the late 1600s at Lloyd's Coffeehouse in London as a means of sharing the risks of commercial voyages. Underwriters received a fee for the portion of the financial responsibility they shouldered.

Although organized insurance first developed with the maritime industry, the need for protection also grew in other areas. Life insurance, first appearing in Philadelphia in 1759, originally was designed to minimize the loss from death by pooling the risk with others. Accident insurance appeared in the United States in the mid-1800s, and automobile insurance appeared in the late 1800s. Today, property and casualty insurance companies in the United States write more than $259 billion in premiums per year.

As the insurance business became more complex, the need for specialized personnel, like claims representatives, developed.

The Job

An insurance company's reputation and success is dependent upon its ability to quickly and effectively investigate claims, negotiate equitable settlements, and authorize prompt payments to policyholders. Claims representatives perform these duties.

Claims clerks review insurance forms for accuracy and completeness. Frequently, this involves calling or writing the insured party or other people involved to secure missing information. After placing this data in a claim file, the clerk reviews the insurance policy to determine coverage. Routine claims are transmitted for payment; if further investigation is needed, the clerk informs the claims supervisor.

In companies specializing in property and casualty insurance, claims adjusters may perform some or all of the duties of claims clerks. They can determine whether the policy covers the loss and amount claimed. Through investigation of physical evidence, the securing of testimony from relevant parties, including the claimant, witnesses, police, and, if necessary, hospital personnel, and the examination of reports, they promptly negotiate a settlement. Adjusters make sure that the settlement reflects the actual claimant losses, while making certain the insurer is protected from invalid claims.

Adjusters may issue payment checks or submit their findings to claims examiners for payment. If litigation is necessary, adjusters recommend this action to legal counsel, and they may attend court hearings.

Most claims adjusters specialize in one type of insurance. They act exclusively in one field, such as fire, marine, automobile, or product liability. For example, a *claims agent for petroleum* handles activities connected with locating, drilling, and producing oil or gas on private property. In states with "no fault" insurance, adjusters are not concerned with responsibility, but they still must determine the amount of payment. To help settle automobile insurance claims, an *automobile damage appraiser* examines damaged cars and other vehicles, estimates the cost of labor and parts, and determines whether it is more practical to make the repairs on the damaged car or to pay the claimant the precollision market value of the vehicle.

For minor or routine claims, the trend among property and casualty insurers is to employ *telephone adjusters* or *inside adjusters*. They use the telephone and written correspondence to gather information, including loss estimates, from the claimant. Drive-in claim centers have developed to provide on-the-spot settlement for minor claims. After determining the loss, the adjuster issues a check immediately.

More complex claims are handled by *outside adjusters*. Outside adjusters spend more time in the field investigating the claim and gathering relevant information.

In life and health insurance companies, *claims examiners* perform all the functions of claims adjusters. Examiners in these companies, and in others where adjusters are employed, review settled claims to make sure the settlements and payments adhere to company procedures and policies. They report on any irregularities. In cases involving litigation, they confer with attorneys. Where large claims are involved, a senior examiner frequently handles the case.

Requirements

High School

Recommended high school courses include typing or word processing, business, and mathematics. Speech and English classes will help workers in this occupation hone their communication skills.

Postsecondary Training

College graduates generally are preferred for insurance claims jobs, but persons with special experience may not need a degree. No specific college major is preferred, but certain ones may indicate a possible specialty. For example, an engineering degree would be valuable in industrial claims, and a legal background would be helpful in claims involving workers' compensation and product liability. In most companies, on-the-job training is usually provided. All insurance claims representatives should be comfortable working with computers, so be sure to hone your computer skills in college.

Supplementary professional education is encouraged by insurance companies. A number of options are available. The Insurance Institute of America offers a series of courses culminating in a comprehensive examination. Passing the exam earns the examinee an Associate in Claims designation. The College of Insurance in New York City offers a program leading to a professional certificate in insurance adjusting. In addition, life and health claims examining programs for people interested in working as claims examiners are offered by both the Life Office Management Association and the International Claim Association; both programs lead to a professional designation.

Certification or Licensing

Most states require licensing of claims representatives. The requirements for licensing vary and may include age restrictions, state residency, education in such classes as loss adjusting or insurance, character references, and written examinations.

Other Requirements

Claims representatives are in a people-oriented profession. They must be able to communicate effectively to gain the respect and confidence of all involved parties. They should be mathematically adept and have a good memory. Knowledge of legal and medical terms and practice, as well as state and federal insurance laws and regulations, is required in this profession. Some companies require applicants to take aptitude tests designed to measure mathematical, analytical, and communication skills.

Exploring

There are many ways to explore this field. You might try to get a summer or part-time entry-level job with an insurance company. This would allow you to see what working in the insurance industry is like. You can also ask your parents, teachers, or a guidance counselor to arrange a tour of an insurance company or at least to set up an information interview with someone who works in the field. Finally, you may consider contacting the various associations that offer educational materials and even sign up for an introductory course to see if this career is for you.

Employers

Insurance companies are the principal employers of processing and claims clerks, adjusters, and appraisers. Others are employed by real estate firms and by the government.

Starting Out

A person interested in this field should contact the personnel departments of insurance companies directly. Positions can also be located in the classified sections of newspapers, on the Internet at industry-related sites, and by using the local office of the U.S. Employment Service Office.

Advancement

Depending upon the individual, advancement prospects are good. As trainees demonstrate competence and advance in coursework, they are assigned higher and more difficult claims. Promotions are possible to department supervisor in a field office or a managerial position in the home office. Sometimes claims workers transfer to underwriting and sales departments.

Earnings

Salaries for those working in the insurance industry vary according to their position, experience, and education. According to the U.S. Department of Labor, insurance claims clerks averaged an annual salary of $24,010 in 1998. The department also reported that insurance adjusters, examiners, and investigators averaged $38,290 that same year. Naturally, supervisors and managers often earned more than this amount, up to $55,000 per year.

Insurance companies usually offer strong fringe benefits, including liberal vacation policies and employer-financed life and retirement programs. Many companies offer telecommuting options—especially for outside claims adjusters.

Work Environment

Inside adjusters work in offices, as do clerks and examiners. They work 35 to 40 hours a week and occasionally travel. They may work additional hours during peak claim periods or when quarterly or annual reports are due. Outside claims adjusters may travel extensively—sometimes hundreds of miles to different states to handle a claim. An adjuster may also be required to be on call 24 hours a day.

Outlook

Growth for this field will be about as fast as the average through 2008, according to the U.S. Department of Labor. Most of the new jobs will be created as a result of increased insurance sales, resulting in a larger number of insurance claims. Jobs will also come from growth in the population, economics, trends in insurance settlement procedures, and opportunities arising from employees who change jobs or retire.

The predominance of the group most in need of protection, individuals between 25 and 54, indicates the need for more claims jobs. Also, as the number of working women rises, so will demand for increased insurance coverage. New and expanding businesses will require insurance for production plants and equipment as well as employees.

Claims representatives who specialize in complex business insurance, such as marine cargo, workers' compensation, and product and pollution liability insurance, will be in demand. Insurance claims representatives will always be in demand since their work requires significant interpersonal contact and does not lend itself to automation.

For More Information

For educational information, contact:

The College of Insurance
101 Murray Street
New York, NY 10007
Tel: 800-356-5146
Web: http://www.tci.edu

Information on health insurance adjusting and continuing education can be obtained from:

Health Insurance Association of America
555 13th Street, NW
Washington, DC 20004
Tel: 202-824-1600
Web: http://www.hiaa.org

For information on the Associate in Claims designation and other educational programs, contact:

Insurance Institute of America
720 Providence Road
PO Box 3016
Malvern, PA 19355-0716
Tel: 800-644-2101
Web: http://www.aicpcu.org

For information on the Associate, Life and Health Claims, and the Fellow, Life Management Institute, designations, contact:

Life Office Management Association
2300 Windy Ridge Parkway, Suite 600
Atlanta, GA 30339-8443
Tel: 800-275-5662
Web: http://www.loma.org

Information on public insurance adjusting can be obtained from:

National Association of Public Insurance Adjusters
112-J Elden Street
Herndon, VA 20170
Tel: 703-709-8254
Email: napia@erols.com
Web: http://www.napia.com/

For information on certification and educational programs in Canada, contact:

Insurance Institute of Canada
18 King Street East, 6th Floor
Toronto, ON M5C 1C4, Canada
Tel: 416-362-8586
Email: genmail@iic-iac.org
Web: http://iic.lasso.net

Insurance Policy Processing Workers

	School Subjects
Business Mathematics	

	Personal Skills
Following instructions Leadership/management	

	Work Environment
Primarily indoors Primarily one location	

	Minimum Education Level
High school diploma	

	Salary Range
$15,660 to $23,960 to $35,380	

	Certification or Licensing
None available	

	Outlook
About as fast as the average	

Overview

Insurance policy processing workers perform a variety of clerical and administrative tasks that ensure that insurance applications and claims are handled in an efficient and timely manner. They review new applications, make adjustments to existing policies, work on policies that are to be reinstated, check the accuracy of company records, verify client information, and compile information used in claim settlement. Insurance policy processing workers also handle business correspondence relating to any of the above duties. They use computers, word processors, calculators, and other office equipment in the course of their work.

History

Organized insurance was first developed in the shipping industry during the late 1600s as a means of sharing the risks of commercial voyages. Underwriters received a fee for the portion of the financial responsibility they covered.

As the need for further protection developed, other types of insurance were created. After the London Fire of 1666, fire insurance became available in England. Life insurance first appeared in the United States in 1759; accident insurance followed in 1863; and automobile insurance was instituted in 1898.

Now, millions of dollars worth of insurance policies are written every day. Skilled claims examiners, medical-voucher clerks, and other insurance workers are needed to process applications and claims accurately and efficiently so clients get the coverage to which they are entitled.

The Job

Insurance policy processing workers are involved in all aspects of handling insurance applications and settling claims (or requests from policy holders regarding payment). The individual policies are sold by an *insurance agent* or *broker*, who sends the policies to processing workers and waits to see whether the company accepts the policy under the terms as written. The agent or the customer may contact policy processing workers many times during the life of a policy for various services. Claims examiners review settled insurance claims to verify that payments have been made according to company procedures and are in line with the information provided in the claim form. These professionals may also need to contact policy processing clerks in the course of reviewing settlements. While a policy processing worker may be assigned a variety of tasks, insurance companies increasingly rely on specialists to perform specific functions.

Claims clerks review insurance claim forms for accuracy and completeness. Frequently, this involves calling or writing the insured party or other people involved to secure missing information. After placing this data in a claims file, the clerk reviews the insurance policy to determine the coverage. Routine claims are transmitted for payment; if further investigation is needed, the clerk informs the claims supervisor.

Claims supervisors not only direct the work of claims clerks but are also responsible for informing policy owners and beneficiaries of the procedures for filing claims. They submit claim liability statements for review by the actuarial department and inform department supervisors of the status of claims.

Reviewers review completed insurance applications to ensure that all questions have been answered by the applicants. They contact insurance agents to inform them of any problems with the applications, and if none are found, reviewers suggest that policies be approved and delivered to policyholders. Reviewers may collect premiums from new policyholders and provide management with updates on new business.

Policy-change clerks compile information on changes in insurance policies, such as a change in beneficiaries, and determine if the proposed changes conform to company policy and state law. Using rate books and a knowledge of specific types of policies, these clerks calculate new premiums and make appropriate adjustments to accounts. Policy-change clerks may help write a new policy with the client's specified changes or prepare a rider to an existing policy.

Cancellation clerks cancel insurance policies as directed by insurance agents. They compute any refund due and mail any appropriate refund and the cancellation notice to the policyholder. Clerks also notify the bookkeeping department of the cancellation and send a notice to the insurance agent.

Revival clerks approve reinstatement of customers' insurance policies if the reason for the lapse in service, such as an overdue premium, is corrected within a specified time limit. They compare answers given by the policyholder on the reinstatement application with those previously approved by the company and examine company records to see if there are any circumstances that make reinstatement impossible. Revival clerks calculate the irregular premium and the reinstatement penalty due when the reinstatement is approved, type notices of company action (approval or denial of reinstatement), and send this notification to the policyholder.

Insurance checkers verify the accuracy and completeness of insurance company records by comparing the computations on premiums paid and dividends due on individual forms. They then check that information against similar information on other applications. They also verify personal information on applications, such as the name, age, address, and value of property of the policyholder, and they proofread all material concerning insurance coverage before it is sent to policyholders.

Insurance agents must apply to insurance companies in order to represent the companies and sell their policies. *Agent-contract clerks* evaluate the ability and character of prospective insurance agents and approve or reject their contracts to sell insurance for a company. They review the prospective agent's application for relevant work experience and other qualifications and check the applicant's personal references to see if they meet company standards. Agent-contract clerks correspond with both the prospective agent and company officials to explain their decision to accept or reject individual applications.

Medical-voucher clerks analyze vouchers sent by doctors who have completed medical examinations of insurance applicants and approve payment of these vouchers based on standard rates. These clerks note the doctor's fee on a form and forward the form and the voucher to the insurance company's bookkeeper or other appropriate personnel for further approval and payment.

Requirements

High School

A high school diploma is usually sufficient for beginning insurance policy processing workers. To prepare yourself for this job, you should take courses in English, mathematics, and computer science while in high school. In addition, take as many business-related courses, such as typing, word processing, and bookkeeping, as possible.

Postsecondary Training

Community colleges and vocational schools often offer business education courses that provide training for insurance policy processing workers. You may want to consider taking these courses to improve your possibilities for advancement to supervisory positions.

Other Requirements

Prospective workers should have some aptitude with business machines, the ability to concentrate for long periods of time on repetitive tasks, and mathematical skills. Legible handwriting is a necessity. Because they often work with policyholders and other workers, insurance policy processing workers must be able to communicate effectively and work well with others. In addition, insurance policy processing workers need to be familiar with state and federal insurance laws and regulations. They should find systematic and orderly work appealing, and they should like to work on detailed tasks.

Other personal qualifications include dependability, trustworthiness, and a neat personal appearance. Insurance policy processing personnel who work for the federal government may need to pass a civil service examination.

Exploring

You can get experience in this field by assuming clerical or bookkeeping responsibilities for a school club or other organization. In addition, some school work-study programs may have opportunities with insurance companies for part-time, on-the-job training. It may also be possible to get a part-time or summer job with an insurance company.

You can get training in office procedures and the operation of business machinery and computers through evening courses offered by business schools. Another way to gain insight into the responsibilities of insurance policy processing workers is to talk to someone already working in the field.

Employers

Insurance companies are the principal employers of insurance policy processing workers. These workers may perform similar duties for real estate firms and the government.

Starting Out

Those interested in securing an entry-level position should contact insurance agencies directly. Jobs may also be located through help-wanted advertisements or by using the local office of the U.S. Employment Service.

Some insurance companies may give potential employees an aptitude test to determine their ability to work quickly and accurately. Work assignments may be made on the basis of the results of this test.

Advancement

Many inexperienced workers begin as file clerks and advance to positions in policy processing. Insurance policy processing workers usually begin their employment handling the more routine tasks, such as reviewing insurance applications to ensure that all the questions have been answered. With experience, they may advance to more complicated tasks and assume a greater responsibility for complete assignments. Those who show the desire and ability may be promoted to clerical supervisory positions, with a corresponding increase in pay and work responsibilities. To become a claims adjuster or an underwriter, it is usually necessary to have a college degree or have taken specialized courses in insurance. Many such courses are available from local business or vocational colleges and various industry trade groups.

The high turnover rate among insurance policy processing workers increases opportunities for promotions. The number and kind of opportunities, however, may depend on the place of employment and the ability, training, and experience of the employee.

Earnings

Insurance policy processing workers' salaries varied depending on such factors as the worker's experience and the size and location of the employer. Generally, those working for large companies in big cities earned higher salaries. According to the U.S. Department of Labor, the median yearly income for insurance policy processing clerks in 1998 was $23,960. In addition, the Research and Statistics Office of the Minnesota Department of Economic Security reported that nationwide the lowest paid 10 percent of these processing clerks earned approximately $15,660, while the highest paid 10 percent made roughly $35,380, also in 1998.

As full-time employees of insurance companies, policy processing workers usually receive the standard fringe benefits of vacation and sick pay, health insurance, and retirement plans.

Work Environment

As is the case with most office workers, insurance policy processing employees work an average of 37 to 40 hours a week. Although the work environment is usually well ventilated and lighted, the job itself can be fairly routine and repetitive, with most of the work taking place at a desk. Policy processing workers often interact with other insurance professionals and policyholders, and they may work under close supervision.

Because many insurance companies offer 24-hour claims service to their policyholders, some claims clerks may work evenings and weekends. Many insurance workers are employed part-time or on a temporary basis.

Outlook

The U.S. Department of Labor predicts the job growth for all insurance processing workers to be about as fast as the average through 2008. The department notes, however, that claims clerk positions will grow faster than other processing positions. Personnel in policy processing who have only clerical duties and no contact with customers may actually face a decline in positions. This decline will be due to the increased use of data processing machines and other types of automated equipment that increase worker productivity and result in the need for fewer workers.

Many jobs will result from workers retiring or otherwise leaving the field. Employment opportunities should be best in and around large metropolitan areas, where the majority of large insurance companies are located. There should be an increase in the number of opportunities for temporary or part-time work, especially during busy business periods.

For More Information

For information on educational programs, contact:

Insurance Institute of America
720 Providence Road
PO Box 3016
Malvern, PA 19355-0716
Tel: 800-644-2101
Web: http://www.aicpcu.org

Insurance Institute of Canada
18 King Street East, 6th Floor
Toronto, ON M5C 1C4, Canada
Tel: 416-362-8586
Email: genmail@iic-iac.org
Web: http://iic.lasso.net

Insurance Underwriters

Business Mathematics	School Subjects
Following instructions Leadership/management	Personal Skills
Primarily indoors Primarily one location	Work Environment
Bachelor's degree	Minimum Education Level
$23,750 to $38,710 to $77,430	Salary Range
Recommended	Certification or Licensing
Little change or more slowly than the average	Outlook

Overview

Insurance underwriters review individual applications for insurance to evaluate the degree of risk involved. They decide whether the insurance company should accept an applicant, and, if the applicant is accepted, underwriters determine the premium that the policyholder will be charged. There are approximately 97,000 underwriters employed in the United States.

History

Lloyd's of London is generally considered to be the first insurance underwriter. Formed in the late 1600s, Lloyd's subscribed marine insurance policies for seagoing vessels. Over the years, the principles of insurance were adopted by various fraternal and trade unions.

In the United States, private insurance companies began to furnish insurance protection in the early 1900s. Insurance companies have grown greatly and expanded since World War II. Today, the U.S. insurance market is second only to Japan in the world with over $600 billion in premiums.

The Job

People buy insurance policies to protect themselves against financial loss resulting from injuries, illnesses, or lost or damaged property; policyholders transfer this risk of loss from themselves to their insurance companies. As a result, insurance companies assume billions of dollars in risks each year. Underwriters are responsible for evaluating the degree of risk posed by each policy application to determine whether the insurance company should issue a policy.

Underwriters base their decisions on a number of factors, including the applicant's health, occupation, and income. They review and analyze information in insurance applications, medical reports, reports from loss control specialists, and actuarial studies. If an applicant appears to be at a greater risk level than normal, the underwriter may decide that an extra premium is needed. Underwriters must exercise sound judgment when deciding whether to accept an applicant and in deciding upon the premium; their decisions are crucial to the financial success of the insurance company.

Insurance underwriting is a very competitive business. If the underwriter evaluates risks too conservatively and quotes prices that are too high, the insurance company may lose business to competitors. If the underwriters evaluate risks too liberally and accept applications at inadequate prices, the company will have to pay more claims and will ultimately lose money. It is essential that underwriters evaluate applications very carefully.

Many underwriters specialize in life, property, or health insurance; many further specialize in individual or group policies. *Property or casualty underwriters* may specialize by the type of risk involved, such as fire or automobile. Some underwriters work exclusively with business insurance. These *commercial account underwriters* must often evaluate the firm's entire business operation.

Group contracts are becoming increasingly popular. In a group policy, life or health insurance protection is given to all persons in a certain group at uniform rates. Group contracts may also be given to specified groups as individual policies reflecting individual needs. A labor union, for example, may be given individual casualty policies covering automobiles.

Underwriters must assess the acceptability of risk from a variety of policy applications. They must be able to review and analyze complex technical information.

Requirements

High School

Small insurance companies may hire people without a college degree for trainee positions, and high school graduates may be trained for underwriting work after working as underwriting clerks. In general, however, a college education is very advantageous. In high school you should take mathematics, business, and speech classes to help prepare you for work in this field. A basic knowledge of computers is also necessary.

Postsecondary Training

Most insurance companies prefer to hire college graduates for beginning underwriting jobs. A degree in any major is acceptable, but a degree in business administration or finance may be particularly helpful. Also, accounting classes and business law classes help to round out your educational background for this field. In addition, keep up your computer skills in college. The computer is a tool you will use throughout your professional career.

Certification or Licensing

Underwriters who work to earn certified, or designated, titles show commitment to their profession and increase their possibilities for advancement. Several designations are available to underwriters. The Insurance Institute of America, for example, offers an Associate in Underwriting (AU) designation. Requirements for the AU include completion of designated course work (usually lasting 2 years) and the passage of a comprehensive examination. The American Institute for Chartered Property Casualty Underwriters offers a more advanced professional certification, the Chartered Property and Casualty Underwriter (CPCU) designation. Course work for the CPCU usually takes 5 years, and a candidate must pass 10 examinations covering such subjects as accounting, finance, business law, and commercial risk management. For life insurance underwriters, The American College offers the Chartered Life Underwriter (CLU) designation. Like the CPCU, the CLU requires completing a comprehensive series of courses and passing examinations.

Other Requirements

Underwriting work requires great concentration and mental alertness. Underwriters must be analytical, logical, and detail oriented. They must be able to make difficult decisions based on technical, complicated information. Underwriters must also be able to communicate well both in speech and in writing. Group underwriters often meet with union employees or employer representatives. The ability to communicate well is vital for these underwriters.

Keep in mind that advancement in this career comes through continuing your education. While insurance companies often pay tuition for their employees taking underwriting courses, the underwriters themselves must have the desire to learn continuously.

Exploring

There are many different ways to explore the underwriting profession. You may visit insurance companies to talk with underwriters and other insurance employees. Many insurance organizations, such as those listed at the end of this article, will send basic information on underwriting jobs to interested people. You might also consider applying for a part-time or summer job at an insurance company.

High school graduates may decide to work at insurance companies before going to college to determine their interest in and aptitude for underwriting work. In addition, many insurance companies are willing to hire and train college students during the summer months.

Employers

Of the approximately 97,000 underwriters in the United States, most work for property and casualty insurance companies. Insurance agents, brokers, and services and life insurance companies are the next two largest employers of underwriters. Opportunities are often best in large cities such as New York, Chicago, San Francisco, Dallas, Philadelphia, and Hartford. Finally, some underwriters work in independent agencies, banks, mortgage companies, or regional offices.

Starting Out

The most effective way to enter the underwriting profession is to seek employment after earning a college degree. Most insurance companies prefer to hire college graduates, and college placement offices often assist students in securing employment.

It is possible to enter this field without a college degree. Underwriting clerks who show exceptional promise may be trained for underwriter positions. In addition, some insurance companies will hire people without a college degree for trainee jobs.

Advancement

Advancement opportunities for underwriters depend on an individual's educational background, on-the-job performance, and leadership abilities. Continuing education is also very important.

Experienced underwriters who have taken continuing education courses may be promoted to chief underwriter or underwriting manager. Underwriting managers may advance to senior management positions.

Earnings

In 1998, according to the U.S. Department of Labor, the median annual salary for underwriters was $38,710. At the low end of the scale, 10 percent of underwriters earned about $23,750 per year. The top 10 percent earned approximately $77,430. Experience, certification, and position within the company are all factors influencing salary levels. In addition, most insurance companies have generous employee benefits, normally including liberal vacation allowances and employer-financed group life and retirement plans.

Work Environment

Underwriters generally work at a desk in pleasant offices; their jobs entail no unusual physical activity, although at times they may have to work under stressful conditions. The normal work week is 35 to 40 hours; overtime may be required from time to time. Occasionally, underwriters may travel away from home to attend meetings or continuing education classes. In general, working conditions are very good for underwriters.

Outlook

The U.S. Department of Labor predicts a slower than average employment outlook for insurance underwriters through 2008. Most job openings will occur as a result of underwriters leaving the field for other professions or retirement. The increasing use of underwriting software programs and the increasing numbers of businesses that self-insure will limit job growth in this field.

There will always be a need for underwriters. New businesses will seek protection for new plants and equipment, insurance for workers' compensation, and product liability. The public's growing security consciousness and the increasing importance of employee benefits will result in more opportunities in this field. And, finally, the increasing number of Americans over the age of 65 who utilize long-term health care and pension benefits will create a demand for underwriters.

For More Information

For information regarding the CLU designation and distance education programs, contact:

The American College
270 South Bryn Mawr Avenue
Bryn Mawr, PA 19010-2196
Tel: 888-263-7265
Email: StudentServices@Amercoll.Edu
Web: http://www.amercoll.edu

For information regarding the CPCU certification, contact:

> **American Institute for Chartered Property Casualty Underwriters**
> 720 Providence Road
> PO Box 3016
> Malvern, PA 19355-0716
> Tel: 800-644-2101
> Web: http://www.aicpcu.org

For information about AU certification as well as general information about the insurance industry and underwriting, contact:

> **Insurance Institute of America**
> 720 Providence Road
> PO Box 3016
> Malvern, PA 19355-0716
> Tel: 800-644-2101
> Web: http://www.aicpcu.org

For information on continuing education and general information about health underwriting, contact:

> **National Association of Health Underwriters**
> 2000 North 14th Street, Suite 450
> Arlington, VA 22201
> Tel: 703-276-0220
> Web: http://www.nahu.org/

For information on life underwriting, contact:

> **National Association of Insurance and Financial Advisors**
> 2901 Telestar Court
> Falls Church, VA 22042-1205
> Tel: 703-770-8100
> Web: http://www.naifa.org

This organization is associated with The American College and has information on industry news and events.

> **Society of Financial Service Professionals**
> 270 South Bryn Mawr Avenue
> Bryn Mawr, PA 19010-2195
> Tel: 610-526-2500
> Web: http://www.financialpro.org

Life Insurance Agents and Brokers

School Subjects
Business
Mathematics

Personal Skills
Communication/ideas
Leadership/management

Work Environment
Primarily indoors
One location with some travel

Minimum Education Level
Some postsecondary training

Salary Range
$17,870 to $34,370 to $91,890+

Certification or Licensing
Required by all states

Outlook
Little change or more slowly
than the average

Overview

Life insurance agents and brokers sell policies that provide life insurance, retirement income, and various other types of insurance to new clients or to established policyholders. Some agents are referred to as *life underwriters*, since they may be required to estimate insurance risks on some policies. Approximately 387,000 insurance agents and brokers work in the United States; about 26 percent of that number specialize in working for life insurance carriers.

History

The first life insurance company in the United States was founded in Philadelphia in 1759 and was known as "A Corporation for the Relief of Poor and Distressed Presbyterian Ministers and of Poor and Distressed Widows and Children of Presbyterian Ministers." The company still exists, although its name has been shortened to the Presbyterian Ministers Fund.

In the middle of the 19th century, companies similar to today's life insurance firms began to develop. Two types of organizations grew: mutual companies, which are owned by the policyholders, and stock companies, which are owned by stockholders. The emergence of the profession of full-time insurance agent, who is paid a commission on the basis of what is sold, contributed greatly to the growth of life insurance.

The Job

Life insurance agents act as field sales representatives for the companies to which they are under contract. They may be under direct contract or work through a general agent who holds a contract. Insurance brokers represent the insurance buyer and do not sell for a particular company but place insurance policies for their clients with the company that offers the best rate and coverage. In addition, some brokers obtain several types of insurance (automobile, household, medical, and so on) to provide a more complete service package for their clients.

The agent's work may be divided into five functions: identifying and soliciting prospects, explaining services, developing insurance plans, closing the transaction, and following up.

The life insurance agent must use personal initiative to identify and solicit sales prospects. Few agents can survive in the life insurance field by relying solely on contacts made through regular business and social channels. They must make active client solicitation a part of their regular job. One company, for example, asks that each agent make between 20 and 30 personal contacts with prospective customers each week, through which 8 to 12 interviews may be obtained, resulting in from 0 to 3 sales. As in many sales occupations, many days or weeks may pass without any sales, then several sales in a row may suddenly develop.

Some agents obtain leads for sales prospects by following newspaper reports to learn of newcomers to the community, births, graduations, and business promotions. Other agents specialize in occupational groups, selling to physicians, farmers, or small businesses. Many agents use general telephone or mail solicitations to help identify prospects. All agents hope that satisfied customers will suggest future sales to their friends and neighbors.

Successful contact with prospective clients may be a difficult process. Many potential customers already may have been solicited by a number of life insurance agents or may not be interested in buying life insurance at a particular time. Agents are often hard-pressed to obtain their initial goal—a personal interview to sit down and talk about insurance with the potential customer.

Once they have lined up a sales interview, agents usually travel to the customer's home or place of business. During this meeting, agents explain their services. Like any other successful sales pitch, this explanation must be adapted to the needs of the client. A new father, for example, may wish to ensure his child's college education, while an older person may be most interested in provisions dealing with retirement income. With experience, agents learn how best to answer questions or objections raised by potential customers. The agents must be able to describe the coverage offered by their company in clear, nontechnical language.

With the approval of the prospective client, the agent develops an insurance plan. In some cases, this will involve only a single standard life insurance policy. In other instances, the agent will review the client's complete financial status and develop a comprehensive plan for death benefits, payment of the balance due on a home mortgage if the insured dies, creation of a fund for college education for children, and retirement income. Such plans usually take into account several factors: the customer's personal savings and investments, mortgage and other obligations, Social Security benefits, and existing insurance coverage.

To best satisfy the customer's insurance needs, and in keeping with the customer's ability to pay, the agent may present a variety of insurance alternatives. The agent may, for example, recommend term insurance (the cheapest form of insurance since it may only be used as a death benefit) or ordinary life (which may be maintained by premium payments throughout the insured's life but may be converted to aid in retirement living). In some cases, the agent may suggest a limited payment plan, such as 20-payment life, which allows the insured to pay the policy off completely in a given number of annual premiums. Agents can develop comprehensive life insurance plans to protect a business enterprise (such as protection from the loss resulting from the death of a key partner), employee group insurance plans, or the creation and distribution of wealth through estates. The agent's skill and the variety of plans offered by the company are combined to develop the best possible insurance proposal for customers.

Closing the transaction is probably the most difficult part of the insurance process. At this point, the customer must decide whether to purchase the recommended insurance plan, ask for a modified version, or conclude that additional insurance is not needed or affordable.

After a customer decides to purchase a policy, the agent must arrange for him or her to take a physical examination; insurance company policies require that standard rates apply only to those people in good health. The agent also must obtain a completed insurance application and the first premium payment and send them with other supporting documents to the company for its approval and formal issuance of the policy.

The final phase of the insurance process is follow-up. The agent checks back frequently with policyholders both to provide service and to watch for opportunities for additional sales.

Successful life insurance agents and brokers work hard at their jobs. A majority of agents average over 40 hours of work a week. Because arranging a meeting often means fitting into the client's personal schedule, many of the hours worked by insurance agents are in the evenings or on weekends. In addition to the time spent with customers, agents must spend time in their homes or offices preparing insurance programs for customer approval, developing new sources of business, and writing reports for the company.

Requirements

High School

Formal requirements for the life insurance field are few. Because more mature individuals are usually better able to master the complexities of the business and inspire customer confidence, most companies prefer to hire people who are at least 21 years of age. Many starting agents are more than 30 years of age. If this field interests you, there are a number of courses you can take in high school to prepare yourself for college and this type of work. Naturally you should take English classes. These classes will help you improve your research, writing, and possibly speaking skills—all communication skills that you will use in this line of work. If your high school offers economics or finance classes, take these as well. Working with insurance means working with money and numbers, and these classes will give you this exposure. You may also benefit from taking sociology and psychology classes, which can give you a greater understanding of people. Finally, take math and computer classes. Undoubtedly you will be using computers in your professional life, so start becoming comfortable with this tool now.

Postsecondary Training

Today most insurance companies and agencies prefer to hire college graduates. Those who have majored in economics or business will likely have an advantage in getting jobs. Classes you can take in college that will help you in this field include math, economics, and accounting. Business law, government, and business administration classes will help you understand the functions of different types of insurance as well as learn how to successfully run a business. Of course, keep up with your computer work. Knowing how to use software, such as spreadsheet software, will be indispensable in your line of work. You may want to attend a college or university that offers specific courses in insurance; there are more than 60 colleges and universities in the United States that offer such classes.

Certification or Licensing

Life insurance agents must obtain a license in each state in which they sell insurance. Agents are often sponsored for this license by the company they represent, which usually pays the license fee.

In most states, before a license is issued, the agent must pass a written test on insurance fundamentals and state insurance laws. Companies usually provide training programs to help prepare for these examinations. Often, the new agent may sell on a temporary certificate while preparing for the written examination. Information on state life insurance licensing requirements can be easily obtained from the state commissioner of insurance. Agents that sell securities, such as mutual funds, must obtain a separate securities license.

For full professional status, many companies recommend that their agents become chartered life underwriters (CLU) and/or chartered financial consultants (ChFC). To earn these designations, agents must successfully complete at least three years of work in the field and course work offered through The American College. This work will demonstrate the agents' ability to apply their knowledge of life insurance fundamentals, economics, business law, taxation, trusts, and finance to common insurance problems. The CLU and ChFC designations are awarded by The American College in Bryn Mawr, Pennsylvania. Only a small percentage of life insurance agents are CLUs and/or ChFCs.

Other Requirements

Personal characteristics of agents are of great importance. The following traits are most helpful: a genuine liking and appreciation for people; a positive attitude toward others and sympathy for their problems; a personal belief in the value of life insurance coverage; a willingness to spend several years learning the business and becoming established; and persistence, hard work, and patience. Sales workers should also be resourceful and organized to make the most effective use of their time.

Requirements for success in life insurance are elusive, and it is this fact that contributes to the high turnover rate in this field. Despite the high rate of failure, life insurance sales offers a rewarding career for those who meet its requirements. It has been said that life insurance offers the easiest way to earn $1,000 to $2,000 a week, but the most difficult way to earn $300 or $400. People with strong qualifications may readily develop a successful insurance career, but poorly qualified people will find it a very difficult field.

Exploring

Because of state licensing requirements, it is difficult for young people to obtain actual experience. The most notable exceptions are the student-agency programs developed by several companies to provide college students with practical sales experience and a trial exposure to the field.

Those wishing to learn about life insurance may be able to get a part-time or summer job as a clerical worker in an insurance agency. This work will provide background information on the requirements for the field and an understanding of its problems and prospects for the future. Formal college or evening school courses in insurance will also provide a clearer picture of this profession's techniques and opportunities.

Employers

Life insurance agents and brokers can be found throughout the country, but most work in or near large cities. The majority work out of local offices or in independent agencies; others are employed at insurance company headquarters.

Starting Out

Aspiring agents may apply directly to personnel directors of insurance companies or managers of branches or agencies. In most cases, the new agent will be affiliated with a local sales office almost immediately. To increase the agency's potential sales volume, the typical insurance office manager is prepared to hire all candidates who can be readily recruited and properly trained. Prospective life insurance agents should discuss their career interests with representatives of several companies to select the employer that offers them the best opportunities to fulfill their goals.

Prospective agents should carefully evaluate potential employers to select an organization that offers sound training, personal supervision, resources to assist sales, adequate financial compensating, and a recognizable name that will be well received by customers. Students graduating from college should be able to arrange campus interviews with recruiters from several insurance companies. People with work experience in other fields usually find life insurance managers eager to discuss sales opportunities.

In addition to discussing personal interests and requirements for success in the field, company representatives usually give prospective agents aptitude tests, which are developed either by their company or by LIMRA International (formerly the Life Insurance Marketing and Research Association).

Formal training usually involves three phases. In precontract orientation, candidates are provided with a clearer picture of the field through classroom work, training manuals, or other materials. On-the-job training is designed to present insurance fundamentals, techniques of developing sales prospects, principles of selling, and the importance of a work schedule. Finally, intermediate instruction usually provides company training of an advanced nature.

More than 30,000 agents a year take the insurance courses prepared by the Life Underwriter Training Council (LUTC). After completing a certain number of courses, an agent may apply for the professional educational designation of life underwriter training council fellow, which is awarded jointly by LUTC and the National Association of Insurance and Financial Advisors.

Advancement

Continuing education has become essential for life insurance agents. Several professional organizations offer courses and tests for agents to obtain additional professional certification. Although voluntary, many professional insurance organizations require agents to commit to continuing education on a regular basis. Membership in professional organizations and the accompanying certification is important in establishing client trust. Many states also require continuing education to maintain licensing.

Unlike some occupations, many of the ablest people in the life insurance field are not interested in advancing into management. There can be many reasons for this. In some cases, a successful sales agent may be able to earn more than the president of the company. Experienced agents often would rather increase their volume of business and quality of service rather than their responsibility for the work of others. Others develop by specializing in various phases of insurance.

Still, many successful agents aspire to positions in sales management. At first, they may begin by helping train newcomers to the field. Later, they may become assistant managers of their office. Top agents are often asked by their companies (or even by rival insurance companies) to take over as managers of an existing branch or to develop a new one. In some cases, persons entering management must take a temporary salary cut, particularly at the beginning, and may earn less than successful agents.

There are several types of life insurance sales office arrangements. *Branch office managers* are salaried employees who work for their company in a geographic region. *General agency managers* are given franchises by a company and develop and finance their own sales office. *General agents* are not directly affiliated with their company, but they must operate in a responsible manner to maintain their right to represent the company. *General insurance brokers* are self-employed persons who place insurance coverage for their clients with more than one life insurance company.

The highest management positions in the life insurance field are in company headquarters. Persons with expertise in sales and field management experience may be offered a position with the home office.

Earnings

According to the U.S. Department of Labor, in 1998 the median yearly income of insurance agents and brokers was about $34,370. The department also reported that the lowest paid 10 percent of these workers, which typically includes those just beginning in the field, made approximately $17,870. The highest paid 10 percent earned $91,890 or more. Many offices also pay bonuses to agents that sell a predetermined amount of coverage. Beginning agents usually receive some form of financial assistance from the company. They may be placed on a moderate salary for a year or two; often the amount of salary declines each month on the assumption that commission income on sales will increase. Eventually, the straight salary is replaced by a drawing account—a fixed dollar amount that is advanced each month against anticipated commissions. This account helps agents balance out high- and low-earning periods.

Agents receive commissions on two bases: a first-year commission for making the sale (usually 55 percent of the total first-year premium) and a series of smaller commissions paid when the insured pays the annual premium (usually 5 percent of the yearly payments for nine years). Most companies will not pay renewal commissions to agents who resign.

Annual earnings of agents vary widely, from the beginning agent who may sell one policy a month up to the approximately 20,000 agents each year who qualify for the "Million Dollar Round Table" by selling policies with a face value of more than $1 million.

Work Environment

The job of the life insurance agent is marked by extensive contact with others. Most agents actively participate in groups such as churches, synagogues, community groups, and service clubs, through which they can meet prospective clients. Life insurance agents also have to stay in touch with other individuals to keep their prospective sales list growing.

Because they are essentially self-employed, agents must be self-motivated and capable of operating on their own. In return, the life insurance field offers people the chance to go into business for themselves without the need for capital investment, long-term debt, and personal liability.

When asked to comment on what they liked least about the life insurance field, a group of experienced agents listed the amount of detail work required of an agent, the lack of education by the public concerning life insurance, the uncertainty of earnings while becoming established in the field, and the amount of night and weekend work. The last point is particularly important. Some agents work four nights a week and both days of the weekend when starting out. After becoming established, this may be reduced to three or two evenings and only one weekend day. Agents are often torn between the desire to spend more time with their families and the reality that curtailing evening and weekend work may hurt their income. Most agents work a 40 hour week, although those beginning in the field and those with thriving businesses may work longer, some up to 60 hours.

Outlook

The U.S. Department of Labor predicts little change in job growth for insurance agents and brokers through 2008. Despite this little change, however, there should be opportunities for people with the right skills. The percentage of citizens older than 65 is growing at a much faster rate than that of the general population. Agents will be needed to meet the special needs of this group, converting some insurance policies from a death benefit to retirement income. Also, the 25 to 54 age group is growing. This is the age group that has the greatest need for insurance, and agents will be needed to provide them with services. In addition, more women in the workplace will increase insurance sales. Finally, employment opportunities for life insurance agents will be aided by the general increase in the nation's population, the heavy turnover among new agents, and the openings created by agents retiring or leaving the field.

A number of factors may contain job growth in this field. For example, some life insurance business has been taken over by multiline insurance agents who handle every type of insurance, thus reducing the need for those specializing in selling life insurance. Department stores and other businesses outside the traditional insurance industry have begun to offer insurance. Also, customer service representatives are increasingly assuming some sales functions, such as expanding accounts and occasionally generating new accounts. Many companies are diversifying their marketing efforts to include some direct mail and telephone sales. Increased use of computers will lessen the workload of agents by creating a database for tailor-made policies. Rising productivity among existing agents also will hold down new job openings. In addition, the life insurance industry has come under increasing competition from financial institutions that offer retirement investment plans such as mutual funds.

For More Information

The American College is the nation's oldest distance learning institution for financial service education. For information regarding the CLU and ChFC designations, contact:

The American College
270 South Bryn Mawr Avenue
Bryn Mawr, PA 19010-2195
Tel: 610-526-1000
Web: http://www.amercoll.edu

This is the nation's oldest and largest independent agent association. For job information, contact:

Independent Insurance Agents of America, Inc.
127 South Peyton Street
Alexandria, VA 22314
Tel: 800-221-7917
Email: info@iiaa.org
Web: http://www.independentagent.com/

For information on insurance aptitude tests, contact:

LIMRA International
300 Day Hill Road
Windsor, CT 06095
Tel: 860-688-3358
Web: http://www.limra.com

For information on continuing education, contact:

National Association of Insurance and Financial Advisors
2901 Telestar Court
Falls Church, VA 22042-1205
Tel: 703-770-8100
Web: http://www.naifa.org

Property and Casualty Insurance Agents and Brokers

	School Subjects
Business Mathematics Speech	
	Personal Skills
Communication/ideas Leadership/management	
	Work Environment
Primarily indoors Primarily one location	
	Minimum Education Level
Some postsecondary training	
	Salary Range
$17,870 to $34,370 to $91,890+	
	Certification or Licensing
Required by all states	
	Outlook
Little change or more slowly than the average	

Overview

Property and casualty insurance agents and brokers sell policies that help individuals and companies cover expenses and losses from such disasters as fires, burglaries, traffic accidents, and other emergencies. These salespeople also may be known as *fire, casualty, and marine insurance agents or brokers*. There are about 387,000 insurance agents and brokers employed in the United States. Approximately 13 percent of those agents and brokers work specifically for property and casualty insurance carriers.

History

The development of the property and casualty insurance industry parallels the history of human economic development. This type of insurance was first established in the maritime field. A single shipwreck could put a ship owner out of business, so it became essential for trade financiers to share this risk. Organized maritime insurance began in the late 17th century at Lloyd's coffeehouse in London, where descriptions of individual ships, their cargoes, and their destinations were posted. Persons willing to share the possible loss, in return for a fee, signed their names below these descriptions indicating what percentage of the financial responsibility they were willing to assume. Those who signed were known as "underwriters," a term still used in the insurance business.

As people became more experienced in this procedure, predictions of loss became more accurate and rates were standardized. To provide protection for larger risks, individuals organized companies. The first marine insurance company in the United States—the Insurance Company of North America—was founded in Philadelphia in 1792 and still does business today.

Other types of insurance developed in response to people's need for protection. Insurance against loss by fire became available after the disastrous lesson of the London Fire of 1666. The first accident insurance policy in the United States was sold in 1863. Burglary insurance—protection against property taken by forced entry—was offered soon thereafter. Theft insurance, which covers any form of stealing, was first written in 1899.

Around the turn of the century, the development of the "horseless carriage" led to the automobile insurance industry. The first automobile policy was sold in 1898. This area of the insurance field grew rapidly. In the mid-1990s premiums written for automobile insurance (including liability and collision and comprehensive policies) totaled more than $102 billion.

Growth of business and industrial organizations required companies to offer protection for employees injured on the job. The first workers' compensation insurance was sold in 1910.

Insurance companies have always been alert to new marketing possibilities. In the past few decades, increasing emphasis has been placed upon "package" policies offering comprehensive coverage. A typical package policy is the homeowner's policy which, in addition to fire protection for the insured's home and property, also covers losses for liability, medical payments, and additional living expenses. In the mid-1950s, a group of private firms provided the first insurance on the multimillion-dollar reactors used in atomic energy plants.

Over the course of the past decade, costs associated with the property and casualty insurance industry (including underwriting losses) have outstripped the annual rate of inflation. This has generally led to an increase in the premium rates charged to customers. The largest increases have occurred in the automobile insurance sector of the industry. The overall trend reflects some basic changes in American society, including a substantial rise in crime and litigation and the development of expensive new medical technologies. The main challenge of the property and casualty insurance industry in the coming years is to stabilize premium rates to remain competitive with alternative forms of risk financing.

The Job

Property and casualty insurance salespeople work under one of two types of relationships with insurers and clients. An agent serves as an authorized representative of the insurance company or companies with which the agent has a contract. A broker, on the other hand, serves as the representative for the client and has no contracts with insurance companies.

Agents can be *independent agents, exclusive agents,* or *direct writers.* Independent agents may represent one or more insurance companies, are paid by commission, are responsible for their own expenses, and own the rights to the policies they sell. Exclusive agents represent only one insurance company, are generally paid by commission, are generally responsible for all of their own expenses, and usually own the rights to the policies that they sell. Direct writers represent only one insurance company, are employees of that company (and therefore are often paid a salary and are not responsible for their own expenses), and do not own the rights to the policies that are owned by the company.

Regardless of the system that is used, salespeople operate in a similar fashion. Each one orders or issues policies, collects premiums, renews and changes existing coverage, and assists clients with reports of losses and claims settlement. Backed by the resources of the companies that they represent, individual agents may issue policies insuring against loss or damage for everything from furs and automobiles to ocean liners and factories.

Agents are authorized to issue a "binder" to provide temporary protection for customers between the time they sign the policy application and the policy is issued by the insurance company. Naturally, the agent must be selective in the risks accepted under a binder. Sometimes a risk will be refused by a company, which might cause the agent to lose goodwill with the customer.

Since brokers do not directly represent or have contracts with insurance companies, they can not issue binders.

Some agents or brokers specialize in one type of insurance such as automobile insurance. All agents or brokers, however, must have a knowledge of the kind of protection required by their clients and the exact coverage offered by each company that they represent.

One of the most significant aspects of the property and casualty agent's work is the variety encountered on the job. An agent's day may begin with an important conference with a group of executives seeking protection for a new industrial plant and its related business activities. Following this meeting, the agent may proceed to the office and spend several hours studying the needs of the customer and drafting an insurance plan. This proposal must be thorough and competitively priced because several other local agents will likely be competing for the account. While working at the office, the agent usually receives several calls and visits from prospective or current clients asking questions about protection, policy conditions, changes, or new developments.

At noon, the agent may attend a meeting of a service club or have lunch with a policyholder. After lunch, the agent may visit a garage with a customer to discuss the car repairs needed as the result of a client's automobile accident. Back at the office, the agent may talk on the telephone with an adjuster from the insurance company involved.

In the late afternoon, the agent may call on the superintendent of schools to discuss insurance protection for participants and spectators at athletic events and other public meetings. If the school has no protection, the agent may evaluate its insurance needs and draft a proposed policy.

Upon returning to the office, the agent may telephone several customers, dictate responses to the day's mail, and handle other matters that have developed during the day. In the evening, the agent may call on a family to discuss insurance protection for a new home.

Requirements

High School

Insurance companies typically insist that their agents have at least a high school degree, and most strongly prefer their agents to have a college education. There are a number of classes you can take in high school to prepare yourself both for college and for working in the insurance industry. If your high school offers business, economics, or finance classes, be sure to take advantage of these courses. Mathematics classes will also give you the opportunity to develop your skills working with numbers, which is an important aspect of insurance work. Computer courses will allow you to become familiar with this technology, a technology that you will use throughout your career. In order to develop your communication skills—an essential for any salesperson—take English and speech classes. Finally, consider taking classes that will give you insight into people's actions, which is another important skill for a salesperson. Psychology and sociology classes are courses that may offer this opportunity.

Postsecondary Training

Although college training is not a prerequisite for insurance work, those who have a college degree in economics or business will probably have an advantage starting out in this field. Many colleges and universities offer courses in insurance, and a number of schools offer a bachelor's degree in insurance. Classes you are likely to take in college include finance, accounting, and economics. Business law and business administration classes will give you an understanding of legal issues and insurance needs. Also, psychology courses may help you to increase your understanding of people. Finally, keep up with your computer work. Courses that teach you to use software, such as spreadsheet software, will keep your skills up-to-date and make you more marketable. For some specialized areas of property insurance, such as fire protection for commercial establishments, an engineering background may prove helpful.

Certification or Licensing

All agents and brokers must obtain licenses from the states in which they sell insurance. Most states require that the agent pass a written examination dealing with state insurance laws and the fundamentals of property and casualty insurance. Often, candidates for licenses must show evidence of some formal study in the field of insurance.

Those agents who wish to seek the highest professional status may pursue the designation of Chartered Property Casualty Underwriter (CPCU). The CPCU requires the agent to complete at least 3 years in the field successfully, demonstrate high ethical practices in all work, and pass a series of 9 examinations offered by the American Institute for Chartered Property and

Casualty Underwriters. Agents and brokers may prepare for these examinations through home study or by taking courses offered by colleges, insurance associations, or individual companies. As an intermediate step, many agents complete a study and examination program conducted by the Insurance Institute of America. One such program leads to the designation Accredited Adviser in Insurance (AAI). To earn the AAI designation an agent must pass 3 national exams. Although independent study for the AAI is possible, most agents participate in classes given at a state independent agents' association prior to taking the exams.

Other Requirements

An agent or broker must thoroughly understand insurance fundamentals and recognize the differences between the many options provided by various policies. This knowledge is essential for the salesperson to gain the respect and confidence of clients. To provide greater service to customers and increase sales volume, beginning agents must study many areas of insurance protection. This requires an analytical mind, the ability to teach oneself how to use standard manuals and computer information systems, as well as the capacity for hard work.

Successful agents and brokers are able to interact with strangers easily and talk readily with a wide range of people. For example, an agent or broker may need to talk with teenagers about their first cars, with business executives faced with heavy responsibilities, or with widows confronted for the first time with financial management of a home. Agents must be resourceful, self-confident, conscientious, and cheerful. As in other types of sales occupations, a strong belief in the service being sold helps agents to be more successful in their presentations.

Because they spend so much of their time with others, agents must have a genuine liking for people. Equally important is the desire to serve others by providing financial security. To be successful, agents must be able to present insurance information in a clear, nontechnical fashion. They must be able to develop a logical sales sequence and presentation style that is comfortable for prospects and clients.

Successful agents usually participate in a number of social activities, such as religious groups, community organizations, and service organizations. They must stay visible within their communities to keep their volume of business up. It is essential that people respond positively to them. They often have an unusual facility for recalling people's names and past conversations they've had with them.

Because they work in small organizations, agents must possess both personal sales and management abilities. Many insurance offices consist of the agent and a single secretary. The freedom enjoyed by the agent necessitates discipline and careful self-planning.

Exploring

Because of state licensing requirements, it is sometimes difficult for young people to obtain part-time experience in this field. Summer employment of any sort in a property and casualty insurance office may give you helpful insights into the field. Since many offices are small and must have someone on premises during business hours, you may find summer positions with individual agencies or brokerage firms. Colleges with work-study programs may offer opportunities for practical experience in an insurance agency.

Employers

Insurance companies are the principal employers of property and casualty insurance agents and brokers. Other agents and brokers—approximately 30 percent—are self-employed.

Starting Out

College graduates are frequently hired through campus interviews for salaried sales positions with major companies. Other graduates secure positions directly with local agencies or brokerages through placement services, employment offices, or classified advertisements in newspapers. Many high school and college graduates apply directly to insurance companies. Sometimes persons employed in other fields take evening or home-study courses in insurance to prepare for employment in this field.

Once hired, the new agent or salesperson uses training materials prepared by the company or by industry trade groups. In smaller agencies, newcomers may be expected to assume most of the responsibility for their own training by using the agency's written resources and working directly with experienced agents. In larger organizations, initial training may include formal classroom instruction and enrollment in education programs such as those offered by the Insurance Institute of America. Sometimes insurance societies sponsor courses designed to help the beginning agent. Almost all agents receive directed, on-the-job sales supervision.

Advancement

Sales agents may advance in one of several ways. They may decide to establish their own agency or brokerage firm, join or buy out an established agency, or advance into branch or home office management with an insurance company.

Self-employed agents or brokers often remain with the organization that they have developed for the length of their careers. They may grow professionally by expanding the scope of their insurance activities. Many agents expand their responsibilities and their office's sales volume by hiring additional salespeople. Occasionally an established agent may enter related areas of activity. Many property insurance agents, for example, branch out into real estate sales. Many agents and brokers devote an increasing amount of their time to worthwhile community projects, which helps to build goodwill and probable future clients.

Earnings

Recently hired sales agents are usually paid a moderate salary while learning the business. After becoming established, however, most agents are paid on the basis of a commission on sales. Agents who work directly for an insurance company often receive a base salary in addition to some commission on sales production. Salespeople employed by companies often receive fringe benefits (such as retirement income, sick leave, and paid vacations), whereas self-employed agents or brokers receive no such benefits.

According to the U.S. Department of Labor, the median annual salary for all types of insurance agents and brokers was $34,370 in 1998. At that same time, the lowest paid 10 percent of agents made approximately $17,870. The highest paid 10 percent, which typically included those with the most experience and largest clientele, earned $91,890 or more.

Unlike life insurance agents, who receive a high first-year commission, the property and casualty agent usually receives the same percentage each time the premium is paid.

Work Environment

Property and casualty insurance agents must be in constant contact with people—clients, prospective clients, and the workers in the home office of the insurance companies. This can be very time-consuming, and occasionally frustrating, but it is an essential element of the work.

Two of the biggest drawbacks to this type of work are the long hours and irregular schedule. Agents often are required to work their schedules around their clients' availability. Especially in their first years in the business, agents may find that they have to work three or four nights a week and one or two days on the weekend. Most agents work 40 hours a week, but some agents, particularly those just beginning in the field and those with a large clientele, may work 60 hours a week or more.

Outlook

The employment rate of all insurance agents and brokers is expected to show little change through 2008, according to the U.S. Department of Labor. Nevertheless, individuals with determination and the right skills should have numerous job opportunities for several reasons. The overall demand for insurance should be strong as the general population grows and the amount of personal and corporate possessions rises. Most homeowners and business executives budget insurance as a necessary expense. Their dependence on insurance coverage is reflected in the fact that insurance premium rates have gone up about 100 percent in the past 10 years. In addition, laws that require businesses to provide workers' compensation insurance and car owners to obtain automobile liability protection help to maintain an insurance market.

A number of factors, however, are responsible for restraining job growth of insurance agents and brokers. Computers enable agents to perform routine clerical tasks more efficiently, and more policies are being sold by mail and phone. Also, as insurance becomes more and more crucial to their financial health, many large businesses are hiring their own risk managers, who analyze their insurance needs and select the policies that are best for them.

There is a high turnover in this field. Many beginning agents and brokers find it hard to establish a large, profitable client-base, and they eventually move on to other areas in the insurance industry. Most openings will occur as a result of this turnover and as workers retire or leave their positions for other reasons.

For More Information

For information regarding the CPCU designation, continuing education courses, and industry news, contact:

American Institute for Chartered Property and Casualty Underwriters
720 Providence Road
PO Box 3016
Malvern, PA 19355-0716
Web: http://www.aicpcu.org

For information on scholarships and women in the insurance industry, contact:

Association of Professional Insurance Women
PO Box 98
Church Street Station
New York, NY 10008
Email: Info@apiw.org
Web: http://www.apiw.org

For information on the industry and educational opportunities, contact:

Independent Insurance Agents of America
127 South Peyton Street
Alexandria, VA 22314
Email: info@iiaa.org
Web: http://www.independentagent.com/

For information on the AAI designation and other educational programs, contact:

Insurance Institute of America
720 Providence Road
PO Box 3016
Malvern, PA 19355-0716
Web: http://www.aicpcu.org

Risk Managers

Economics Mathematics	School Subjects
Communication/ideas Leadership/management	Personal Skills
Primarily indoors One location with some travel	Work Environment
Bachelor's degree	Minimum Education Level
$27,680 to $55,070 to $150,000	Salary Range
Recommended	Certification or Licensing
About as fast as the average	Outlook

Overview

Risk managers help businesses control risks and losses while maintaining the highest production levels possible. They work in industrial, service, non-profit, and public-sector organizations. By protecting a company against loss, the risk manager helps it to improve operating efficiency and meet strategic goals.

History

Entrepreneurs have always taken steps to prevent losses or damage to their businesses. Only since the mid-1950s, however, has risk management developed into a specialized field. During the Industrial Revolution, business owners recognized that as production levels increased, risks increased at the same rate. The risks were often managed at the expense of worker health and safety.

With the rapid growth of technology came greater and more varied risks. Risk management changed from simply buying insurance against risks, to planning a wide variety of programs to prevent, minimize, and finance losses.

The Job

Risk management protects people, property, and inventory. For example, factories that use hazardous chemicals require employees to wear protective clothing; department stores use closed-circuit surveillance to minimize shoplifting and vandalism; and manufacturers have a plan of action to follow should their products injure consumers. The five general categories of risks are damage to property, loss of income from property damage, injury to others, fraud or criminal acts, and death or injury of employees.

Risk managers first identify and analyze potential losses. They examine the various risk management techniques and select the best ones, including how to pay for losses that may occur. After the chosen techniques are implemented, they closely monitor the results.

Risk management has two basic elements: risk control and risk finance. Risk control involves loss prevention techniques to reduce the frequency and lower the severity of losses. Risk managers make sure operations are safe. They see that employees are properly trained and that workers have and use safety equipment. This often involves conducting safety and loss prevention programs for employees. They make recommendations on the safe design of the workplace, and make plans in case of machinery breakdowns. They examine company contracts with suppliers to ensure a steady supply of raw materials.

Risk finance programs set aside funds to pay for losses not anticipated by risk control. Some losses can be covered by the company itself; others are covered by outside sources, such as insurance firms. Risk finance programs try to reduce costs of damage or loss, and include insurance programs to pay for losses.

Large organizations often have a risk management department with several employees who each specialize in one area, such as employee-related injuries, losses to plant property, automobile losses, and insurance coverage. Small organizations have risk managers who may serve as safety and training officers in addition to handling workers' compensation and employee benefits.

Requirements

High School

If you are interested in becoming a risk manager, you should plan on getting a bachelor's degree and may at some point consider getting an advanced degree, such as Master's of Business Administration (MBA) or a Master's in Risk Management. In high school, therefore, you should take classes that will prepare you for college as well as help you explore this type of work. Take plenty of mathematics classes. Also, take accounting, business, and economics if your school offers these classes. To round out your education, take a variety of science, history, government, and computer classes. And of course, take English classes, which will hone your research and writing skills and make you ready for college-level work.

Postsecondary Training

Risk managers generally need a college degree with a broad business background. Depending on the college or university you attend, you may be able to major in risk management or insurance. There are about 100 schools that offer courses or degrees in insurance and risk management. If your school does not offer these degrees, consider a major in other management or finance areas, such as accounting, economics, engineering, finance, law, management, or political science. No matter what your particular major, your class schedule will most likely include economics, accounting, and mathematics, such as calculus. Computer classes that deal with using a variety of software programs will also be necessary to take. Insurance and even banking classes will give you an understanding of these industries and the financial tools they use.

Certification or Licensing

Many organizations require their risk managers to have an MBA and certification as an Associate in Risk Management (ARM) or the Canadian Risk Management (CRM) designation. The Risk and Insurance Management Society, Inc. offers both ARM and CRM certifications. Requirements for these designations include the completion of 3 graduate-level courses and 3 examinations.

The Risk and Insurance Management Society, Inc. also offers an advanced designation in risk management. The Fellow in Risk Management (FRM) consists of 10 courses—the first 3 from ARM or CRM, with the additional 7 courses focusing on advanced issues in business, insurance, and risk management. Candidates must also pass an examination, sign off on a Code of Ethics, and complete continuing education requirements.

Other Requirements

Communications skills are important for risk managers. They must regularly interact with other departments, such as accounting, engineering, finance, human resources, environmental, legal, research and development, safety, and security. They must also be able to communicate with outside sources, such as attorneys, brokers, union officials, consultants, and insurance agents.

Risk managers must have analytical and problem-solving skills in order to foresee potential problem situations and recommend appropriate solutions. They must be able to examine and prepare reports on risk costs, loss statistics, cost-versus-benefit data, insurance costs, and depreciation of assets.

A knowledge of insurance fundamentals and risk financing is necessary. Risk managers must know loss-control issues such as employee health, worker and product safety, property safeguards, fire prevention, and environmental protection.

Management skills help risk managers set goals, plan strategies, delegate tasks, and measure and forecast results. Computer skills and familiarity with business law are also very helpful.

Exploring

You may wish to ask your family's insurance agent to help you contact a colleague who has commercial accounts and might introduce you to a risk manager for one of their larger clients.

The Risk and Insurance Management Society, Inc.(RIMS), is the largest organization for risk managers, with more than 7,700 individuals in 90 chapters in the United States and Canada. It offers books, monographs, a bimonthly newsletter, education programs, and an annual conference. Students may be able to attend local chapter meetings. The Spencer Educational Foundation, affiliated with RIMS, provides annual scholarships to academically outstanding full-time students of risk management and insurance. (See end of article for contact information.)

Employers

Airlines, banks, insurance companies, manufacturers, government agencies, municipalities, hospitals, retailers, school districts, and universities employ risk managers.

Starting Out

College placement offices can put students in touch with recruiting officers from industries that employ risk managers. Recent graduates can also send resumes to employers of risk managers, such as corporations, service providers, government agencies, and other public and private organizations. Some risk managers join insurance companies, insurance brokerage firms, or consulting firms that provide risk management services to clients.

Some individuals gain experience and education while working in accounting or personnel departments and later move into risk management positions.

Advancement

There is good potential for advancement in the risk management field. Many risk managers work in a related field, such as in a human resources department handling employee benefits.

Risk managers may eventually head a personnel or finance department, become a human resources director, or join the insurance industry. Some become independent consultants. Membership in professional associations that offer networking opportunities can lead to better positions in the field.

Risk managers usually hold mid-level management positions, and often report to a financial officer. Some, however, become vice presidents or presidents of their organizations.

Earnings

Risk managers' salaries vary depending on level of responsibility and authority, type of industry, organization size, and geographic region. The U.S. Department of Labor, which classifies risk managers with financial managers, reported a median yearly income for financial managers of $55,070 in 1998. The lowest paid 10 percent earned approximately $27,680 per year, while the highest paid 10 percent made $118,950 or more. In 1999 an article in *U.S. News and World Report* reported that risk managers holding vice president positions had a salary range of $90,000 to $150,000. Typically, risk managers who work for government agencies earn less than other risk managers. According to the U.S. Department of Labor, financial managers who worked for local government, excluding education and hospital positions, made a median annual income of approximately $48,700 in 1997.

Risk managers usually receive benefits, bonuses, paid vacation, health and life insurance, pensions, and stock options.

Work Environment

Risk managers work in a variety of settings from schools, stores, and government agencies to manufacturers and airlines. Most work in offices, not on the production line, but they may be required to spend some time in production departments. They may have to travel to study risks in other companies or to attend seminars.

Risk managers usually work a 40-hour week, Monday through Friday. They may have to spend much of their time at a computer, analyzing statistics and preparing reports.

Outlook

Since advanced technology continues to increase productivity as well as the potential for disaster, the need for risk management will continue to grow. Organizations now recognize risk management as an integral and effective tool for cost-containment. The profession will continue to gain recognition in the next decade, so salaries and career opportunities are expected to continue to escalate. The U.S. Department of Labor predicts the growth rate for financial managers (including risk managers) to be about as fast as the average through 2008. In a 1999 article, *U.S. News and World Report* listed risk managers as a "hot job," which suggests a strong future for this profession.

For More Information

The American Risk and Insurance Association's goal is to further the science of risk and insurance through education, research, literature, and communications. The Association also offers student membership.

American Risk and Insurance Association
716 Providence Road
PO Box 3028
Malvern, PA 19355-0728
Tel: 610-640-1997
Web: http://www.aria.org/

The Public Risk Management Association has industry news and training programs for risk managers employed in municipal and state governments.

Public Risk Management Association
1815 North Fort Myer Drive, Suite 1020
Arlington, VA 22209-1805
Tel: 703-528-7701
Web: http://www.primacentral.org

For information on continuing education, internships, the ARM, CRM, and FRM designations, and student membership, contact:

Risk and Insurance Management Society, Inc.
655 Third Avenue
New York, NY 10017
Tel: 212-286-9292
Web: http://www.rims.org/

Tax Preparers

School Subjects
Business
Mathematics

Personal Skills
Following instructions
Helping/teaching

Work Environment
Primarily indoors
Primarily one location

Minimum Education Level
Some postsecondary training

Salary Range
$19,500 to $27,510 to $39,050

Certification or Licensing
Required by certain states

Outlook
About as fast as the average

Overview

Tax preparers prepare income tax returns for individuals and small businesses for a fee, either for quarterly or yearly filings. They help to establish and maintain business records to expedite tax preparations and may advise clients on how to save money on their tax payments. There are approximately 79,000 tax preparers employed in the United States.

History

President Franklin D. Roosevelt (1882-1945) once said, "Taxes are the dues that we pay for the privileges of membership in an organized society." Although most people grumble about paying income taxes and filling out tax forms, everyone carries a share of the burden, and it is still possible to keep a sense of humor about income taxes. As Benjamin Franklin (1706-90) succinctly said, "In this world nothing can be said to be certain, except death and taxes."

While the personal income tax may be the most familiar type of taxation, it is actually a relatively recent method for raising revenue. To raise funds for the Napoleonic Wars between 1799 and 1816, Britain became the first nation to collect income taxes, but a permanent income tax was not established there until 1874. In the same manner, the United States first initiated a temporary income tax during the Civil War. It wasn't until 1913, however, with the adoption of the 16th Amendment to the Constitution, that a tax on personal income became the law of the nation. In addition to the federal income tax, many states and cities have adopted income tax laws. Income taxes are an example of a "progressive tax," one that charges higher percentages of income as people earn more money.

Technology has now made it possible to file taxes electronically. Electronic tax filing is a method by which a tax return is converted to computer readable form and sent via modem to the Internal Revenue Service. Electronically filed tax returns are more accurate than paper filed returns because of the extensive checking performed by the electronic filing software. Detecting and correcting errors early also allows the tax return to flow smoothly through the IRS, speeding up the refund process. New computer software is also available which gives individuals a framework in which to prepare and file their own taxes.

The Job

Tax preparers help individuals and small businesses keep the proper records to determine their legally required tax and file the proper forms. They must be well acquainted with federal, state, and local tax laws, and use their knowledge and skills to help taxpayers take the maximum number of legally allowable deductions.

The first step in preparing tax forms is to collect all the data and documents that are needed to calculate the client's tax liability. The client has to submit documents such as tax returns from previous years, wage and income statements, records of other sources of income, statements of interest and dividends earned, records of expenses, property tax records, and so on. The tax preparer then interviews the client to obtain further information that may have a bearing on the amount of taxes owed. If the client is an individual taxpayer, the tax preparer will ask about any important investments, extra expenses that may be deductible, contributions to charity, and insurance payments; events such as marriage, childbirth, and new employment are also important considerations. If the client is a business, the tax preparer may ask about capital gains and losses, taxes already paid, payroll expenses, miscellaneous business expenses, and tax credits.

Once the tax preparer has a complete picture of the client's income and expenses, the proper tax forms and schedules needed to file the tax return can be determined. While some taxpayers have very complex finances that take a long time to document and calculate, others have typical, straightforward returns that take less time. Often the tax preparer can calculate the amount a taxpayer owes, fill out the proper forms, and prepare the complete return in a single interview. When the tax return is more complicated, the tax preparer may have to collect all the data during the interview and perform the calculations later. If a client's taxes are unusual or very complex, the tax preparer may have to consult tax law handbooks and bulletins.

Computers are the main tools used to figure and prepare tax returns. The tax preparer inputs the data onto a spreadsheet, and the computer calculates and prints out the tax form. Computer software can be very versatile and may even print up data summary sheets that can serve as checklists and references for the next tax filing.

Tax preparers often have another tax expert or preparer check their work, especially if they work for a tax service firm. The second tax preparer will check to make sure the allowances and deductions taken were proper and that no others were overlooked. They also make certain that the tax laws are interpreted properly and that calculations are correct. It is very important that a tax preparer's work is accurate and error-free, and clients are given a guarantee covering additional taxes or fines if their work is found to be incorrect. Tax preparers are required by law to sign every return they complete for a client, along with providing their Social Security number or federal identification number. They must also provide the client with a copy of the tax return and keep a copy in their own files.

Requirements

High School

Although there are no specific postsecondary educational requirements for tax preparers, you should certainly get your high school diploma. While you are in high school there are a number of classes you can take that will help prepare you for this type of work. Naturally, take mathematics classes. Accounting, bookkeeping, and business classes will also give you a feel for working with numbers and show you the necessity for accurate work. In addition, take computer classes. You will need to be comfortable using computers since much tax work is done using this tool. Finally, take English classes. English classes will help you work on your research, writing, and speaking skills—important communcation skills to have when you work with clients.

Postsecondary Training

Once you have completed high school, you may be able to find a job as a tax preparer at a large tax preparing firm. These firms, such as H & R Block, typically require their tax preparers to complete a training program in tax preparation. If you would like to pursue a college education, many universities offer individual courses and complete majors in the area of taxation. Another route is to earn a bachelor's degree or master's degree in business administration with a minor or concentration in taxation. A few universities offer master's degrees in taxation.

In addition to formal education, tax preparers must continue their professional education. Both federal and state tax laws are revised every year, and the tax preparer is obligated to understand these new laws thoroughly by January 1 of each year. Major tax reform legislation can increase this amount of study even further. One federal reform tax bill can take up thousands of pages, and this can mean up to 60 hours of extra study in a single month to fully understand all the intricacies and implications of the new laws. To help tax preparers keep up with new developments, the National Association of Tax Practitioners offers more than 200 workshops every year. Tax service firms also offer classes explaining tax preparation to both professionals and individual taxpayers.

Certification or Licensing

Licensing requirements for tax preparers vary by the state, and you should be sure to find out what requirements there are in the state where you wish to practice. Since 1983, for example, tax preparers in California have been required to register with the state Department of Consumers. Tax preparers who apply for registration in that state must be at least eighteen years old and have a high school diploma or the equivalent. In addition, they need to have 60 hours of formal, approved instruction in basic income tax law, theory, and practice, or two years of professional experience in preparing personal income tax returns.

The Internal Revenue Service offers an examination for tax preparers. Those who complete the test successfully are called enrolled agents and are entitled to legally represent any taxpayer in any type of audit before the IRS or state tax boards. (Those with five years' experience working for the IRS as an auditor or in a higher position can become enrolled agents without taking the exam.) The four-part test is offered annually and takes two days to complete. There are no education or experience requirements for taking the examination, but the questions are roughly equivalent to those asked in a college course. Study materials and applications may be obtained from local IRS offices. The IRS does not oversee seasonal tax preparers, but local IRS offices may monitor some commercial tax offices.

To be eligible to process returns and transmit them directly to the Internal Revenue Service via modem, tax preparers must apply to the IRS to become an Electronic Return Originator. A background check and fingerprinting may be required.

The Institute of Tax Consultants offers an annual open book exam to obtain the title of Certified Tax Preparer. Certification also requires 30 hours of continuing education each year.

Other Requirements

Tax preparers should have an aptitude for math and an eye for detail. They should have strong organizational skills and the patience to sift through documents and financial statements. The ability to communicate effectively with clients is also key to be able to explain complex tax procedures and to make customers feel confident and comfortable. Tax preparers also need to work well under the stress and pressure of deadlines. They must also be honest, discreet, and trustworthy in dealing with the financial and business affairs of their clients.

Exploring

If a career in tax preparation sounds interesting, you should first gain some experience by completing income tax returns for yourself and for your family and friends. These returns should be double-checked by the actual taxpayers who will be liable for any fees and extra taxes if the return is prepared incorrectly. You can also look for internships or part-time jobs in tax service offices and tax preparation firms. Many of these firms operate nationwide, and extra office help might be needed as tax deadlines approach and work becomes hectic. The IRS also trains people to answer tax questions for its 800-number telephone advisory service; they are employed annually during early spring.

Try also to familiarize yourself with the tax preparation software available on the Internet and utilize Web sites to keep abreast of changing laws, regulations, and developments in the industry. The National Association of Tax Practicioners offers sample articles from its publication, *Tax Practitioners Journal*, online. (See end of article for contact information.)

Employers

Tax preparers may work for tax service firms such as H & R Block and other similar companies that conduct most of their business during tax season. Other tax preparers may be self-employed and work full or part time.

Starting Out

Because tax work is very seasonal, most tax firms begin hiring tax preparers in December for the upcoming tax season. Some tax service firms will hire tax preparers from among the graduates of their own training courses. Private and state employment agencies may also have information and job listings as will classified newspaper ads. You should also consult your school guidance offices to establish contacts in the field.

There are a large number of Internet sites for this industry, many of which offer job postings. Many large tax preparation firms, such as H & R Block, also have their own Web pages.

Advancement

Some tax preparers may wish to continue their academic education and work toward becoming certified public accountants. Others may want to specialize in certain areas of taxation, such as real estate, corporate, or nonprofit work. Tax preparers who specialize in certain fields are able to charge higher fees for their services.

Establishing a private consulting business is also an option. Potential proprietors should consult with other self-employed practitioners to gain advice on how to start a private practice. Several Internet sites also give valuable advice on establishing a tax business.

Earnings

According to the 1998 edition of the *O*Net Dictionary of Occupational Titles*, the yearly income for tax preparers was approximately $19,500. The Economic Research Institute reported that in 1999 the average starting annual salary for tax preparers was $27,510. Those with 10 years of experience reported an average yearly income of approximately $39,050. Incomes can vary widely from these figures, however, due to a number of factors. One reason is that tax preparers generally charge a fee per tax return, which may range from $30 to $1,500 or more, depending on the complexity of the return and the preparation time required. Therefore, the number of clients a preparer has as well as the difficulty of the returns can affect the preparer's income. Another factor affecting income is the amount of education a tax preparer has. Seasonal or part-time employees, typically those with less education, usually earn minimum wage plus commission. Enrolled agents, certified public accountants, and other professional preparers, typically those with college degrees or more, usually charge more. Finally, it is important to realize that fees vary widely in different parts of the country. Tax preparers in large cities and in the western United States generally charge more, as do those who offer year-round financial advice and services.

Work Environment

Tax preparers generally work in office settings which may be located in neighborhood business districts, shopping malls, or other high traffic areas. Employees of tax service firms may work at storefront desks or in cubicles during the three months preceding the April 15 tax-filing deadline. In addition, many tax preparers work at home to earn extra money while they hold a full-time job.

The hours and schedules that tax preparers work vary greatly, depending on the time of year and the manner in which they are employed. Because of the changes in tax laws that occur every year, tax preparers often advise their clients throughout the year about possible ways to reduce their tax obligations. The first quarter of the year is the busiest time, and even part-time tax preparers may find themselves working very long hours. Workweeks can range from as little as 12 hours to 40 or 50 or more, as tax preparers work late into the evening and on weekends. Tax service firms are usually open seven days a week and 12 hours a day during the first three months of the year. The work is demanding, requiring heavy concentration and long hours sitting at a desk and working on a computer.

Outlook

The U.S. Department of Labor predicts that employment for tax preparers will grow as fast as the average for all other occupations through 2008. According to the IRS, 53 percent of U.S. taxpayers prepare their own returns, but because tax laws are constantly changing and growing more complex, demand for tax professionals will remain high. Much of this demand, however, is expected to be met by the tax preparers already working because computers are increasingly expediting the process of tabulating and storing data. Recent surveys of employers in large metropolitan areas have found an adequate supply of tax preparers; prospects for employment may be better in smaller cities or rural areas.

Although tax laws are constantly evolving and people look to tax preparers to save time, money, and frustration, new tax programs and online resources are easing the process of preparing taxes, lessening the need for outside help. Information is available at the touch of a button on tax laws and regulations. Tax tips are readily available as are online seminars and workshops.

The IRS currently offers taxpayers and businesses the option to "e-file," or electronically file their tax returns on the Internet. While some people may choose to do their own electronic filing, the majority of taxpayers will still rely on tax preparers—licensed by the IRS as Electronic Return Originators—to handle their returns.

For More Information

For training programs, contact:

H & R Block
Tel: 800-472-5625
Web: http://www.hrblock.com

For information on the Certified Tax Preparer designation, contact:

Institute of Tax Consultants
7500 212th SW, Suite 205
Edmonds, WA 98026
Tel: 425-774-3521
Web: http://taxprofessionals.homestead.com/welcome.html

Check out the IRS Web site for information on becoming an enrolled agent or an Electronic Return Originator.

Internal Revenue Service (IRS)
Department of Treasury
Web: http://www.irs.ustreas.gov/prod/cover.html

For industry information, contact:

National Association of Tax Consultants
PO Box 90996
Portland, OR 97290
Tel: 800-745-6282
Web: http://www.natctax.org/main.asp

For information on educational programs, publications, and online membership, contact:

National Association of Tax Practitioners
720 Association Drive
Appleton, WI 54914-1483
Tel: 800-558-3402
Email: natp@natptax.com
Web: http://www.natptax.com/

Index